THE GIRLS

WITH THE

GRANDMOTHER FACES

THE GIRLS

WITH THE

GRANDMOTHER FACES

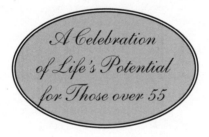

*A Celebration
of Life's Potential
for Those over 55*

FRANCES WEAVER

with incidental drawings from the author's sketchbook

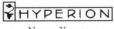

HYPERION

NEW YORK

Library of Congress Cataloging-in-Publication Data
Weaver, Frances.
    The girls with the grandmother faces : a celebration of life's potential for those over 55 / by Frances Weaver.—Rev. ed.
        p.   cm.
    ISBN 0-7868-6169-X
    1. Middle aged women—United States—Life skills guides.
    2. Widows—United States—Life skills guides. 3. Single women—United States—Life skills guides. I. Title.
    HQ1059.5.U5W35   1996
    305.24´2—dc20   95-14579
                                                         CIP

Paperback ISBN 0-7868-8199-2

Designed by Claudyne Bianco Bedell

10 9 8 7 6 5 4 3 2

When in the Course of Human Events . . .

The others my age are all talking "retire"
While I'm just getting a start.
My friends are ready to hang it all up
And I'm just shifting from "park."
My family's all shouting, "Go after it, Mom!"
My mother says, "Why should you go?"
Back off a bit, folks—let me find my own way!
It's years since I've wanted to grow!

I'm lucky as hell just to see the brass ring,
To find a direction—a role—
A way to play catch-up now my other work's done
And I'm free to consider a goal.
A room of my own, as Virginia Woolf said,
Where I can be thinking aloud
While my whole world looks on as I seek my own place.
I just hope to God they'll be proud!

Contents

Introduction

WHO PAINTED ME INTO
THIS CORNER?

*M*iss Sarah ought to know better by now. At least, that's what I thought when I heard about Sarah and her girl friends getting her new car stuck in the mud down by the river.

My youngest grandchild, Sarah, turned seventeen last year. She has nearly finished her junior year in high school with perfect grades and other admirable achievements. But she had a fit when her father had quite a lot to say about driving down on the river banks in melting snow.

"He acts like it's my fault," snarled Sarah.

"Now, don't make her feel guilty. This happens to everyone at that age," her mother urged as Dad fumed.

A family squabble—and I sat trapped in the midst of it!

Grandmothers should keep their mouths shut, I know, so I did—almost.

Finally, the words just had to come out.

"Fault does not apply here. Forget the guilt part. Sarah has been guilty of nothing more than making the wrong choice. And Sarah should be responsible for the results of her choices. Of course, you as parents chose to provide a four-wheel-drive vehicle, which challenges every driver. Of course, you as parents chose to turn Sarah loose with her friends. All of you made these choices. Now you're all bitching and blaming."

I did not say all that quite as well as I have written it. After all, I have had plenty of time to polish that speech to record it for you. I did, however, at that very moment, wish I had had that much insight when Sarah's dad and his brothers were teen-agers. My husband used the words "poor judgment" a lot. I generally resorted to tirades that heaped guilt on the entire family and questioned the sanity of the whole bunch.

All I would have needed, actually, was the realization of the importance of choice. The value of choice. The long-lasting, ever-widening meaning of the choices we make.

What follows here amounts to nothing more than personal opinion. But watching and listening to other women, particularly, convinces me of a basic fact: Right or wrong, good or bad, most of our life's experiences can be traced back to our own choices.

You are shaking your head. "This woman is nuts. I did not choose my own parents, to begin with. I have not chosen my own teachers or the people I work with. I did not choose to have my husband spend every day off watching football or griping about the kids. I did not choose to have neighbors I cannot stand or friends I cannot trust."

True. What you and I *have* chosen is our responses, our reactions. Therein lies the message.

A beat-down-looking woman sat across from me in a meeting aimed at personal growth and all that stuff. Basically, she could have come from Central Casting as the pathetic housewife. Her first and foremost complaint (which we expected, although we did not know her that well) concerned her estranged husband.

"He really knows how to push my buttons," she finally whined.

A quiet voice interrupted. "Of course. After all, he installed those buttons." Laughter died quickly as the speaker continued, "And you chose him for the job."

Months have passed since I heard that exchange. More and more it makes sense to me. There's the truth, folks, and we can make it work for us in our lives.

During my growing years I spent a lot of time mad at my mother. Not so much with my dad, because he wasn't at home a lot. Mother made me practice the piano. Mother wouldn't allow me to wear lipstick. Mother insisted on knee socks—after Easter, even. Mother made me come straight home after school. Mother never approved of the boys I thought were cute. Byword in our house: just don't upset Mother.

Later, Mother told me how to raise my kids, arrange my kitchen, treat my husband, sort the laundry, and lengthen my skirts. Where was my choice?

I—now, get this—I chose to do as she said in order to avoid her famous temper tantrums. Period. I chose to "mind." Just to avoid the possibility of another one of those "Go ahead, make a fool of yourself, hang out with those people, be that kind of a girl, I'm just your mother, God gave me to you so you'd know right from wrong, but I'm only your mother, go ahead, but remember—"

So I chose to do as she said. Don't tell me what would have happened if I had chosen a confrontation. That's history. Now when I feel myself making a choice, it helps to think of that, however. Am I making a positive move here, or am I just avoiding one more scene?

Whatever my reason or justification for any choice, the responsibility for the results, personal or public, will sit on my shoulders. I did that. As much as I might comfort myself by blaming my parents or my husband (convenient, since they're no longer around to argue the point), the choice remains mine.

Now, the flip side.

Gazing back on those years, even fleetingly, we often overlook the great choices we *have* made. Positive changes in our lives have resulted from wise and wondrous decisions we have made.

My choice—and yours?—of a husband worked out better than some marriages have. We have chosen well along the way. So let's give ourselves credit. "Looking for someone with good sense?" we can ask. "Try me."

One of the worst choices is not choosing at all. We know that. Some of our most tedious, boring, or downright traumatic experiences have come from choosing not to choose. We don't have to put on our Hitler imitations or impersonate the Wicked Witch of the West, but we do owe it to ourselves and our world to make decisions and live with the results.

Widowhood—
A Different Kind of Single

THE GIRLS WITH THE
GRANDMOTHER FACES

*N*ot many years ago, I was in the middle of a busy morning. Sarah was tagging along, helping me around the house.

"What're you doin', Grandma?"

"I'm straightening the living room. The girls are coming for bridge this afternoon."

"What girls, Grandma?" By now the kid was jumping on the couch.

"You know, Sarah. The girls I play bridge with on Wednesdays. My friends—"

"Yeah, yeah. I know!" she crowed. "You mean the girls with the grandmother faces."

*T*hose girls are my peer group, my generation. We constitute the fastest-growing segment of our population. Women over fifty-five have more discretionary buying power, better health, better housing, more freedom to move around, more opportunities for continuing education, more leisure time, more labor-saving devices, more knowledge of the world around us, than any single group in the history of the world. Ever.

We also have twenty per cent of our lives still ahead of us, with choices available for improving the quality of our lives as never before. We are, in a very real sense, blessed by the world in which we live.

It is to these women, the girls with the grandmother faces, that this book is primarily addressed. Why? Why would a kite-crazy housewife from Beulah, Colorado ("a little mining town in the West"), feel compelled to write a book pointing out the advantages of being old? Why doesn't this dingbat woman take life easy, lunch at the club, work on the church bazaars, rest on the laurels of her surgeon-hero husband, or look for a new husband, instead of leaving her family two thousand miles behind, starting college all over, and launching a new career just when the rest of us are ready to throw in the towel?

When I was turning forty, I watched the sixty-year-old women I knew best, including my mother. I had first envied these women because they had all of the advantages I was waiting for—grown children with established families of their own, leisure time every time of the day since they no longer cooked for a family, kept house for five or six messy kids, ran errands from dawn to dusk from the orthodontist to the Y, or had mud-stained jeans or football uniforms to contend with. Those women had time to do all of the things I wish I could do now, I thought.

Then I took a closer look. Listened to what those older women were saying. I heard nothing but complaints.

"Life is such a bore, now the kids are grown. I have nothing to do. And they never call home except for money."

"TV is just terrible. Except for *Jeopardy* and *Days of Our Lives,* there's nothing to watch."

"I'd like to take a trip, but we have to go where George can play golf. Which I don't do, of course."

"Cooking for the two of us is stupid."

"I guess Jack's wife is a nice-enough girl, but they never have time for me. You'd think after John died . . ."

"Here we have this wonderful place in Palm Springs and the children refuse to come out here to see us, even for Christmas."

For Pete's sake! I wanted to yell at them. You have all the time and the freedom in the world. What about all those gripes you had about never having time for yourself?

Avoiding those pitfalls of boredom and stagnation became a crusade with me. No way would I let myself get into a rut or lose my enthusiasm for the world around us. Too much is at stake—the rest of our lives.

So this book is addressed to the women my age, widowed or married, who are intrigued by the possibility of changing lifestyles to take advantage of opportunities. For the risk-takers of our world I offer suggestions, to those fearful of making decisions I offer en*courage*ment. (Look at the middle of that word.) To those of you who want to make more of your lives in this important period, I offer hope.

Most important to all of us is attitude. The sincere desire to lead a productive, interesting life at any age depends upon our own imagination and acceptance of new ideas.

How do you know you can't operate a word processor?

How do you know you can't go back to the classroom?

How do you know there's no room for you in the "outside world"?

What makes you so sure you cannot play a guitar or speak Spanish or paint a landscape?

What convinces you that you can't travel on your own? Drive across the country with your grandkids?

The best resource any of us has is ourselves. I have used my own experience as primary research for this book. To my adventures as a runaway grandmother-kiteflier-student-writer-traveler I have added expert advice from wise friends and family members including my mother. I have also read and quoted from authorities on aging.

This book has been fun for me to write. I hope it's a joy for you to read.

THE GOOD HOUSEKEEPING
SEAL OF APPROVAL

What was it like, that little-girl world we lived in more than fifty years ago?

How did we picture ourselves as grownups?

What was important?

What did we do?

What did we expect?

By the time I was old enough to go to school, I assumed I would one day be an old lady like my grandmother. It was my intention to be *exactly* like her. But if Grandmother Allison and I could stand side by side today, the only similarity would be our weight. She was a hefty, well-corseted woman. So am I.

Growing up in Kansas, my sisters and I needed only to cross the street to go to Grandmother's. She lived in the old Victorian where my father and his six sisters had been reared. I sat on the same front porch, ate at the same table, played in the same attic, slept on the same sleeping porch, explored the same fruit cellar, swung under the same tree, and swiped the same soft ginger cookies my dad had thrived on. My cousins, some from as far away as Illinois or California, adored Grandmother and her cookies, too; but I believed the proprietary rights to them were mine.

My grandmother was always at home. Except for church circle or meetings of the library board, I cannot recall her going anyplace. Before Grandfather died she traveled with him. There were stereopticon views and album photos of Yellowstone Park and Santa Monica, and page after page of pictures of the family on vacation in Colorado, perched on huge boulders, wearing long skirts and wide hats.

But Grandmother stayed at home when I knew her. Her groceries were delivered. Her doctor made house calls. She did not own or drive a car.

Family gatherings were rituals. Norman Rockwell would have had a field day when the clan swarmed in with assorted cousins accompanied by *their* cousins from the surrounding countryside—Middle America straight from the cover of the *Saturday Evening Post*. I pictured myself in that same setting, being that kind of a grandmother in that kind of a family.

Now here's the most important recollection about my grandmother, which I wanted to emulate the most: She never yelled. I do not think of her as a controlling woman, but we never felt obliged to misbehave to test her. When we ran in the house or quarreled about trifles, she would say, "Hark, hark!" Nothing more.

To me she epitomized a woman totally comfortable with her surroundings, her place in the world. Old age was apparently exactly what she expected it to be. Unruffled, she sat on her porch or in the "middle" room. She taught us to crochet. She read heavy leather-bound books and recited long poems by heart. I knew I'd be just like her, some day.

Fifty years ago, that block where Grandmother lived was populated by single women, all of whom looked old to me. Richard Armour claims, "There's nothing new about old age." In this case he's right: Old women have outnumbered old men for a long time.

The last man to live on the block in my memory was Grandmother's bachelor brother, Uncle Bill, but he didn't last nearly as long as the old girls did. Next door, with her widowed mother, was Daddy's and my first-grade teacher, Miss McDonald. Next to them lived Miss Anna Bukey. Next neighbor was Mrs. Guymon, and so on. We knew all of these women well, mostly because of their front porches. We skated, jumped rope, and raced on bicycles past their houses. They were the old ladies who bought our first Girl Scout cookies.

What kept these women in their homes? Their homes did, I've decided. Before household chores evolved into a few minutes of button-pushing, these women had something to do all day long, as much or as little as they wanted.

Take the laundry, for example. On Monday morning every woman on that block (often with her hired girl) collected everything in the house and dragged it down steep narrow steps to the basement. They shoved the brutishly heavy Maytag over next to the tubs and started running water. They would run water all day long. Piles of clothes, table and bed linens, and towels were sorted all over the floor, which became wet as the day wore on. After the machine was filled with the hottest water, the entire house reeked with the fumes of Fels Naphtha, Rinso, or "P&G."

Grandmother kept a wooden spoon to break up lumps in the soap. Then she'd fill tubs with rinse water and start the wringer routine. Every item went through that wringer three times. Some went 'round and 'round and had to be pulled out; others were bulky enough to pop open the rollers. Water dripped in every direction no matter how carefully the wringer was positioned. All morning long, wet-heavy baskets of sodden towels and sheets were hoisted up the steps to the clothes lines. The basement floor stayed wet until at least Thursday, so the basement smelled damp forever.

Grandmother or Esther, her right hand, spent at least two hours every Monday in the back yard with a mouthful of clothespins, wrestling with wet sheets. Then another two hours in the afternoon, retrieving the clean clothes and linens. This was the day's activity. It needed to be done. They were needed to do it.

To do my laundry, I don't even have to be at home. The same is true of the other household chores. I can cook without being there. Cleaning and ironing are minuscule tasks compared to the heavy housework of Grandmother's generation.

This, to me, is the primary reason my life at seventy is—can be—different from the life I pictured for myself by observing my grandmother.

So what else is new in the past fifty years?

Personal contacts, to start with. The fabric of American life began to disintegrate with the disappearance of the front porch. This is my own observation; don't expect to find it in any learned psychology book. When we moved to the patio in the back yard, then to the TV in the house, we lost important human contacts.

Evenings were a time of sociability up and down Grandmother's block. The older folks sat on their porches while the younger ones stopped by to visit. Lemonade was found on every front stoop in those days. Sometimes we could sit on the porch and listen to the band concert over in the park. Other nights, we went to the park to hear the music and eat popcorn and catch lightning bugs while our parents chatted with their friends sitting in the cars. But we were together with our neighbors.

"My mother always had someone to talk to," my wise friend Michael says. "The vegetable man, the clothes man, the laundry man, the milk man, the guy who sold linens, the Jewel Tea man—she talked to all of them. Now she has maybe the check-out girl at the supermarket and her doctor.

"Nowadays my mother's doctor is supposed to be a listener for all of her complaints—and she's mad at him most of the time because he hasn't time to hear all she wants to say. She needs someone else to talk to as she had when we were growing up.

"I'll never forget the day the man came to our block selling four-way-stretch girdles. That was the biggest day of the year. All the women followed him down the street, watching how long he stayed at every house. My mother misses that."

Michael's mother is no different from most of the oldsters I know. The world I expected to be old in was shaken to its core in the '40s, started to fall apart in the '50s, and nearly capitulated in the '60s—resulting in total transformation by the '70s. My impression of old women from my childish, impressionable years was no longer valid, or even logical.

With automated housekeeping and the acceptance of women in the work force (beginning with Rosie the Riveter), women's attention turned to wider social issues, thence to establishing their own identities.

Establishing her identity never occurred to my grandmother. She knew who she was. Mother's generation, women now in their eighties and nineties, patterned their sixties after their mothers, even though times had changed so dramatically. Being sixty meant being at home on the shelf. Favorite sayings were, "A woman my age should never . . ." or, "I'm too old for . . ." or, "My mother always said . . ." I don't believe they realized they had at least twenty years ahead to spend some way.

Being sixty certainly doesn't mean being at home on the shelf any more. The message is clear: We cannot live like our grandmothers did, nor like our mothers. Women who don't maintain an active interest in the world around them are of no interest to anyone else. Failure to expand our own horizons is certain to lead to an old age of loneliness and boredom.

It's our own fault if we allow that to happen. The most important asset in a woman's life is probably flexibility. That's a fact, ladies.

The world has changed, and so must we, in spite of our childhood dreams of being like Grandma.

IT'S MY TURN, NOW

"*I*t's just that I'm so lonely!

"Like last weekend I went to our cottage at the shore. My son and his family said they'd join me there, but on Saturday morning the phone rang and I knew without answering that they had something to do in town and I'd be at the beach alone where we used to have so many good times. I could hardly stand it!"

Five minutes before she said this, this woman and I had been total strangers in a crowd of strangers. She was trim, well dressed, articulate, but her mouth was pulled down at the corners in self-pity.

I know that gal, I thought. She's one of us—the girls with the grandmother faces.

The others sitting at the luncheon table with us smiled sympathetically.

"We know how hard it is," said the woman next to her. "Adjusting to being a widow sometimes takes a lot of time. Coming along on this trip to Oxford with this Smithsonian crowd is a good start for you."

Mercifully, we were not subjected at that moment to another

recitation of the woes of widowhood. In my circle, these days, that is often the most popular subject, next to aging—which is equally painful for some women.

Later on, after I decided I really liked this little lady from Virginia, I had a chance for a private conversation.

"How long ago did your husband die?"

She was appalled that I would use that terrible word. There seems to be an unwritten law among the conspicuously grieving that "die" is never said right out loud. She expected to be asked, "How long have you been alone?" or, "When did your dear husband pass away?" That's the liturgy of widowhood among older women. They heard someone, sometime, say, "Never say die," and took it literally.

That oblique language is also a means of hiding from the truth. Dying is a fact of life. (The people who tickle me the most are those who say, "If I die . . ." What other plans do they have in mind?) Facing death and the way it completely changes the lives of the survivors is also a fact of life. My new friend needed to know that.

She went back to the subject of the beach cottage and her loneliness.

"Maybe you don't need that cottage any more," I offered. "Maybe it no longer fits into your life. Have you considered selling it, or renting it—that could be nice extra income." She didn't give me time to go into my discourse about the tax advantages of income properties, which is just as well. I don't actually know that much about such things. Instead, she stared as though I had suggested she remove her right arm.

"But, we've had that place at the shore for twenty years! How could I sell it? Allow strangers to move in there with my things—Herb's things? He'd have a fit!"

"It's not Herb's problem any more. Herb died. You didn't. It's your turn to make the decisions. It's your turn, now, to live your life the way you want to. You have yourself to answer to. If you are miserable with some arrangements of your life, *do something* to change them! Nobody else will. You've had months to figure that out—not just the beach house, but expecting your son and his family to keep you company. You're a grownup. Single for the first time in your life. These can honestly be good years. Don't miss out by wallowing in what used to be. Appreciate your life for what it has been and what it can be.

"You've learned a lot about living that you don't even know you know. Surprise yourself. Take charge. Nobody is trying to say your life will be better without your husband, but it will have to be different. That's only common sense."

She finally smiled and we walked on to Worcester College for another class.

*B*elieve me, I don't go around with my soapbox delivering this tirade to every woman I meet. Just to the ones I think can take it. There are a lot of them.

More than half of the women over sixty-five in America are widows. Older women are also the fastest-growing segment of our population. In terms of absolute numbers, that means there are literally millions of women who no longer have husbands.

So why do so many of the widows I meet act as if this "catastrophe" had never happened to anyone but them? Why do some of the brighter ladies have such a tough time accepting their new roles in life?

That's for the psychologists to answer, certainly, but my own deduction is that loss of married life takes away a safety net. We have used our husbands and our families as a shield, a buffer, an excuse for not making our own decisions or recognizing our own capabilities. Younger women have gotten into this "self-fulfillment" business. We who are in our sixties and seventies have not made that commitment to ourselves until we are suddenly on our own. We have to play catch-up.

For years I have been acquainted with a woman who has devoted the past fifteen or twenty years of her life to being a full-time widow. You know the kind—the weepers you dodge between the aisles in the supermarket to avoid meeting. Everyone in town knew her husband. He was a nice guy, had many friends. To hear her tell it, you'd think she was married to a cross between Abraham Lincoln and Francis of Assisi.

When this crybaby traps anyone between the cereal and the dog food, the ritual of sanctification is repeated. Pictures are dragged from her wallet. The cornered listener stands nodding helplessly while the ice cream softens and the minutes tick away. Finally, she goes on her way carefully composing the remorseful look on her otherwise pleasant face.

She pulls the same stunt with bank tellers, clerks, and the man at the dry cleaners. Why? Because she has never put forth the energy or imagination to make a life of her own. She has no real regard for herself. That's very sad.

Another old friend is more direct about her dependence on her husband. Jean had been president of the medical auxiliary. She had two daughters of whom she could be proud. She was active in her church and in community affairs. When her husband died after several heart attacks, vascular surgery, and other such important warning signs that her life was about to change, Jean repeated again and again, "I never was anything but a doctor's wife. Now I'm not even that!"

Now she's lonely and bored. Maybe some day soon she'll change her outlook—start looking out instead of in.

Widowhood is a rite of passage in the strongest sense of the word. Our lives have changed and can never be the same again. The friends, the social life, the financial priorities, our relationships with our children, daily routines and leisure time, the way we eat, and the way we sleep are all new. It's almost like starting over.

"This woman is too critical of widows. She must have been a terrible wife or had a lousy marriage," you're saying to yourself about now. Maybe so, but certainly no woman in her right mind wants her husband to die. Neither would she want him to go on living in pain, an invalid for her own convenience. The human body is a fragile, mortal piece of equipment. We're fools to expect too much of it. Grieving has its place, but it is for the living, not the dead, that most of us grieve. ("I need him so!")

The real danger is in adopting grieving as a way of life. That's a cop-out because you're still making your husband responsible for your own well-being—hanging your life around his neck.

My husband was a man of great compulsions. His work and his patients were intensely important to him. Had he survived the attack that killed him, he probably would have been a cardiac cripple, if not an invalid, for the rest of his life. I wouldn't wish that on my worst enemy, let alone the father of my children—the man with whom I had shared good times and bad times for thirty-four years. I could not make him young again, in perfect health. Nobody could. That's not facing reality.

John Weaver was also a man of monumental faith. At the risk of sounding preachy, so am I. The basic secret of successful living, widowed or not, is serenity to accept the things we cannot change.

One of the women I've admired for years made the remark after the death of her eighty-year-old husband, "Well, I guess I'll just have to accept the fact that he isn't here any more."

What *else* was she going to do? Where are the choices?

The rest of the Serenity Prayer applies particularly well to the shock of finding oneself adrift and alone after losing a spouse, as they say:

Courage to change the things I can. Remember my friend with the beach cottage?

And the wisdom to know the difference.

That's the toughest part.

THIRTY-FOUR YEARS TO GROW ON

I t's necessary to tell my own story here to qualify what I have to say on this subject.

There's nothing startling to tell. My husband was just getting out of the Army, starting medical school, when we were married. The first ten years of our married life were centered on his education and his career. I had a bachelor's degree in medical technology, but my secret plans of becoming important in his professional life vanished with the first baby, eleven months after we were married. After that, my biggest job was keeping the children quiet so Daddy could study, or filling in as both parents when internship, residency, and combat duty in Korea interfered with family life.

Our third child, Ross, was born while John was on active duty in Korea. John never saw Ross until he was a year old. That was okay. We could take a lot in those days. We had one common goal: general surgery.

Understandably, my husband's practice remained the paramount part of our lives even after the training days were over. I never was one of those old-fashioned women who referred to her husband as "doctor." As a matter of fact, however, there were times when I was convinced I needed to present my Blue Cross card to get his attention.

The kids and I lived around him, in a way. I busied myself with civic affairs, politics, the Episcopal ladies, and the Colonial Dames, but the basic decisions, the nitty-gritty of our lifestyle and activities, were governed by John, just as his father had done in the household where he grew up. I was, in effect, a dutiful wife who knew her place, not without resentment—"on days ending in y," as John used to say.

"As John says . . ." or, now, "As John used to say . . ." has been a part of my conversation for years. John was a wise and witty man with his own way of expressing his thoughts. His imprint on our family is unmistakable.

We spent a lot of time at our house laughing. Jokes came easily to all of us. Not simply story-telling but spontaneously funny reactions to ordinary situations. When John was asked by one of his colleagues if he was making plans for retirement, John fairly bellowed. "Hell, no! How many times a week can anyone clean the !@#%*#! garage?"

In the operating room one day John announced to the assembled nurses, technicians, and others, "My wife and I were having a little game in the living room last night and we discovered a new position." Stunned silence and astonished stares greeted this statement, until he explained, "We found out you can put the dominoes back in the box either sideways or lengthwise."

One old patient felt better on the day she said, "Doctor, tell me the truth. I'm going to die. Right?" He took her hand and replied, "Yes, you are, Mrs. Curry, and so am I. But I don't think either one of us will do it today."

Our prize byword for the holidays came from John: "It's Christmas, goddammit! Be pleasant!" I can still see him at dawn in the midst of torn Christmas wrappings, crying kids, and spilled hot chocolate, wondering how Christmas had turned into such bedlam again—and it wasn't even daylight yet.

Compassionate was a good word for that husband of mine, though he often remarked, when family affairs required sympathy and understanding, "I gave at the office." His own description of himself was, "I'm a humanitarian sonofabitch." And he was.

In the late '60s, John ("Dr. Christian") felt so strongly about the spread of communism and the war in Vietnam that he took time off from his practice twice in two years, two months at a time, to serve as a volunteer surgeon in civilian hospitals in Vietnam. On the Mekong Delta he cared for the people of Phu Vinh and was there during the infamous Tet Offensive of 1968.

The people of Pueblo decided they had a local hero when John wrote home asking for supplies for a Vietnamese orphanage. Everyone in town collected diapers, bottles, lotion, clothes, vitamins, and toys to be sent for his distribution. One group even collected old bowling shirts for the refugees. I have a great picture of a tiny Vietnamese man engulfed in a red shirt reading, "Pueblo Brake and Clutch."

The patients and hospital personnel there appreciated their big American doctor. He was called "Bac Si Beau Coups Kilo," which translates to "doctor of many pounds." Back home after these tours of duty with the AMA-sponsored program, John gave speeches and showed slides of the great improvements in sanitation and hospital facilities because of American medical involvement.

He was a born leader and a basically good man. His family lived in his reflected glory.

Death ended our marriage abruptly. John went up to bed before I did one evening more than fifteen years ago. When I went upstairs an hour later, he was dead—no pain, no disability. He would never have to face retirement or perpetual garage-cleaning or other ways he did not enjoy to spend leisure time. He'd never worry about younger surgeons spoiling his magnificent practice. He was fifty-five. So was I.

*T*wo years before this happened, I had started to write for magazines, mostly by accident. This was the one project I had taken on that had my husband's absolute approval. He read much more than I did and was delighted to discover I was literate. It also pleased him that I stayed at home to do this. When my first article about flying kites appeared in *Vogue,* John bragged to his colleagues about it. He had been forced to buy me only a typewriter. His partner had bought his wife a gift shop.

On the day I started to think of myself as a writer, John came home at noon on a Saturday to find me in the kitchen weeping, clutching a letter—really sobbing.

"Now what?"

I showed him the letter, written in the wiggly script of an old woman. "I loved your article in *Vogue* about Beulah, Colorado. It brought back many memories of my college days and my friend . . . who might be dead by now. . . ."

"A stranger!" I blubbered. "An absolute stranger telling me about her friend in Beulah! And I found the old friend and she's not dead and she's going to write to this lady!"

"Fine. Fine. But why are you so torn up about all this?"

"Because I touched somebody. Because something I wrote has

touched a total stranger. Because now I'm a writer! Now I'm a writer!"

I don't think he really understood. How could he? Surgeons touch people all the time. At least he didn't make fun of my crying, and that was nice.

*B*elieving halfheartedly in "signs" has always been a part of my life. Soon after John's death, writing seemed to me to have come into my life in preparation for widowhood. I felt the same way about the purchase we had made of a small house across the road from our home in Beulah. That was certainly the signal for me to move.

During the first year I floundered, made a lot of mistakes. In the first place, I expected my married children, single son, and grand-children to be ever-watchful and available for their widowed mother. When it became obvious they were not going to drive thirty miles from Pueblo to spend Sunday afternoons with me, I told myself it was understandable, with their own family plans. But I roamed around the house and yard feeling very sorry for myself.

It never occurred to me—at first—to call my widowed friends. I wanted my offspring there, in spite of my constant protestations that I could cope with life on my own.

I bought a small condominium in Pueblo, nearer to family and friends. This was primarily a social move. Couples, two or three at a time, were invited for cocktails at my adorable little pad. I thought they had left me off their guest lists because I'd have a long drive home by myself. The grandchildren and my daughters-in-law would drop by after school, I fantasized. In other words, I wanted to make myself the center of everyone's lives, although I would have knocked anyone out of the ball park for suggesting this as my motive.

The ploy did not work. I paced the floor like a caged mother bear in that condo, waiting for the world I had known so recently to beat a path to my door.

No way. I had to turn the corner completely—realize my life would have to change entirely—before I settled down to a satisfying lifestyle of my own making.

Writing, travel, and college courses made it happen.

THE LAUNCHING OF FRAN WEAVER

*I*n this country today among people over sixty-five, fully eighty per cent of the men are married; more than half of the women of their age group are widowed, and most of us live alone. Only one old man in eight lives alone. Accepting these truths as gospel, immutable fact did not come easily. I had never been an active feminist, but the double standard for the over-the-hill gang upset me for a while.

During these first months of widowhood, I truly resented widowers—those men who were invited to every party and were never expected to repay the invitations—those men who could walk confidently into any restaurant and expect a decent table—those men who could ask any woman on the cruise for a dance and walk away—those men who were socially in demand at all times, in all places. Yet they turned their attention to younger women, and the women my age sat at home because a single man is a plus at any party, but a single woman probably needs a ride home. Now, I know this is a fact of life, as surely as the sun sets in the west or Lake George freezes in January.

*A*t the end of my first floundering year I was convinced that physical separation from home for a while—a real change of scene—might be helpful. Except for a couple of writers' conferences and visits to a relative or two, I had never traveled by myself. Well, Frances, I announced to myself one day, it's time for you to find out how grown up you really are. And I booked a thirty-day cruise.

"Are you going *alone?*" My buddy Martha was flabbergasted.

"Yep," I said, bravely, wondering why I should be frightened.

That first outing gave me the answer: There was no reason. There are nice people to meet and new friends to make all over the world. I had only to reach out to others on my own to find a sense of honest identity. Being in a crowd of strangers is bewildering, but my reward far outweighed the initial feeling of being alone. On that ship, I met fellow passengers who would know me only for myself. I was nobody's wife, or mother, or daughter, or committee chairman, or den mother. I was just me. It was up to me to prove myself worth knowing. I had dropped the safety net. It felt good.

Traveling on that cruise ship felt so good, in fact, I wanted to share the experience with other women and older couples. How? During my career as the world's greatest generic chairperson—you find a cause, I'll get a committee—I had served as chairman for fund-raising trips sponsored by the Colonial Dames. I knew how to organize travelers as a volunteer. Why not go through the same motions as a semi-professional?

I called my travel-agent friend, Judy Smith, to announce she had a new employee: me. I also informed her that I would organize and sell group tours for her agency if she would provide expertise on reservations, computers, and do the bookkeeping. My cut was to be twenty per cent of her gross commission. I was responsible for promotion and travel details. Fine.

I literally launched myself as a tour director with a big party at the Pueblo, Colorado, Country Club. Three cruises had been arranged for 1982. First, a trans-Canal cruise in February. Second, a European port-cities cruise in May. Third, a cruise of the Inside Passage to Alaska in August. Writing letters, sending out clever brochures of my own creation, making hundreds of phone calls and personal interviews, I sold sufficient passage on the February and August cruises on Royal Viking Lines to qualify for an agent's rate. Most of my customers were friends, or friends of friends. We had a generally good time. I had found a way to travel at reduced rates and make travel easier for women fearful of going places on their own. I was growing.

The next big step came when I was raving to my youngest son about Adirondack Community College, where I had been one of the panelists for a writers' workshop. My subject had been "Starting to Write After Forty." Again, I was standing on my own two feet.

Matthew listened to my carrying-on about the campus, the school, the people, and finally said, "Don't you hear yourself, Mother? You're not telling *me* to go to that school. You're saying *you* should go to that school." Bless him.

Two thousand miles is a long way away to go to college, but I did it. Right after I returned from the Alaska cruise I headed east. My granddaughter Sarah and I started school the same day. She went to kindergarten, I went to college. Her grades are better than mine, but we each have had a great time.

The send-off for my new college career was a magnificent display of family support. First of all, my mother in her eighties was encouraging about my going off to school. My daughter in Houston was enthusiastic. But it was my sons and their interest in my renewed academic endeavor that impressed me most.

As a farewell gesture, I treated the family to an Italian restaurant the night before my departure. Chris, number one son, insisted on coffee at his house afterward.

Once in Chris and Mary's living room I found myself seated in the big chair, surrounded by children and grandchildren. They wanted to wish me a pleasant journey and hoped I'd have a good time, I thought. No way. There followed a lecture about the advantages and responsibilities of college life—the same speech each of them had heard from their father and me when they had gone off to school!

"Now, don't think you're going to college just to have a good time with your friends."

"Take courses that will be a challenge for you, Mom. Don't stick to the easy stuff. You're not really dumb, you know."

"You'd better have a budget. No need to spend a lot of money on fancy restaurants or more clothes. Your stuff is good enough. Besides, you're already laying out out-of-state tuition."

I was cautioned about getting into too many extracurricular activities too soon, so I promised not to run for homecoming queen 'til the fall of '83.

They stopped short of warning me about unwanted pregnancy.

They did approve of my leasing my Pueblo condominium during my absence. That showed some fiscal responsibility, I suppose, but their skepticism about my ability to handle money surfaced with their attitude about my use of credit cards. Only for emergencies. I decided they'd heard too much from their father about my spending habits.

Midsummer of '82, I had stopped off in the Glens Falls area long enough to find a place to live for my budding new life as a student.

Two rooms at the Nassau Motel on Lake George Road would suffice. The back room was a large bedroom; the front room was everything else. The kitchen was corner cupboards, refrigerator, sink, and stove-top—no oven. A dinette set and four chairs plus a hide-a-bed couch completed the furnishings. The place was new, clean, and efficient except for the minuscule closet.

*T*wo of my sisters agreed to drive east with me in my big move, another supportive effort that I appreciated. We took ten days to mosey across America, stopping along the way to see everything from the arch at St. Louis to Gettysburg and Harpers Ferry. We ate hot fudge sundaes at Hershey and rode the Circle Line cruise around Manhattan Island. When we arrived in the Adirondacks, they thoroughly approved of my living arrangements, which made me feel even better.

Not since John's freshman year in medical school had I lived in such quarters. This added to the sense of adventure a new beginning. I bought a wok and eventually a word processor, which crowded the place considerably, but I loved the new freedom from "things." The living room was barely big enough to seat six people, but I gave supper parties for my new friends and had a marvelous time.

Late in the spring, after seven months at the motel, I found a condominium for rent at Cannon Point on Lake George—necessary because of an impending visit from my mother. One bedroom, one bath, and no view of the lake was all right for a freshman like me, but hardly suitable for house guests. That condominium sealed the deal between Upstate New York and me. I had found my second home "fitting" in every sense of the word.

For ten years I lived part-time in Upstate New York and part-time in Colorado. In the East I was only me, although I insisted each of my children and their spouses visit Lake George to check it out. It's important to understand each other's motives in the family. They approved. That helped. There will be plenty of time when they might have a helpless old woman on their hands, needing care.

In a way, we're all taking turns—for a few years, anyway.

How Old *Is* Old?

*F*ifty is a time of final options, but it is also a culmination, the prime of life, the beginning of seeing how it all turns out. Let there be less marveling at our wonderful preservation and more respect for the maturity of our mind and spirit. After all, the most important mission of a woman's life is not to hold onto her looks. Our mission is the same as a man's . . . to grow up. To ignore that goal is to exclude women from adult responsibility. Fifty is fifty, and to deny that is to deny wisdom, experience and life itself."

These were the words of Jane O'Reilly in the *New York Times* on July 10, 1986. She also said, "This third of my life is for me. These are my final options."

Well, Jane was a mere child of fifty, but her opinions make even more sense at sixty or seventy.

Which brings us to the second subject: aging. Volumes and tomes have been written about aging. It's a popular subject for scientific study and amateur speculation. More and more of us are living longer and longer, so the subject is inexhaustible. The census charts concerning aging are astonishing. We oldsters are the fastest-growing segment of the population. If we weren't so tired we could take over the whole world.

Some writers are more astute about aging than others, of course. One of the best, to my mind, is M. F. K. Fisher, whose book, *Sister Age,* represents the accumulation of observations and opinions about aging that Ms. Fisher has been collecting for a lifetime.

She writes, "The Aging Process is a part of most of our lives, and it remains one we try to ignore until it seems to pounce upon us. We evade all its signals."

How true. We recognize the fact that we live this long because we have not succumbed to smallpox, tuberculosis, or typhoid fever, as we probably would have done in the past century. We also know that nutrition, sanitation, and sterilization have produced healthier oldsters than have been known in past generations.

But we are reluctant to say, "I'm old." When a tactless (I could say mean, or cruel) house guest said to me, "Are you *only* sixty?" I felt like belting her in her dentures.

The focus on youth on television and in every other aspect of our culture makes us almost ashamed to admit how old we are. A Beverly Hills woman I met not long ago was bragging about the one last favor she performed for her ninety-year-old mother when she died. "I had the mortician cut five years off her age on her tombstone."

Now, really.

But we are all living to riper old ages. I have three sisters, and my mother lived to ninety-two. When my mother was starting to complain about some minor detail of our lives, I told her not to worry; in just a few years all of her children will be on Medicare.

That's too true to be funny. It also illustrates the fact that a sixty-year-old woman has at least twenty years to go, so she'd better stay alert and healthy. Someday *my* kids will be this old.

My heroine, M. F. K. Fisher, continues, "What is important, though, is that our dispassionate acceptance of attrition be matched by a full use of everything that has happened in all the long wonderful-ghastly years to free a person's mind from his body . . . to use the experience . . . so that physical annoyances are surmountable in an alert and even mirthful appreciation of life itself."

The key word is "alert."

*O*ne of the most memorable travel experiences I have had was the Smithsonian-Oxford Seminar because of the ages of the participants. Of the more than a hundred Americans living and studying at Worcester College, Oxford, more than half were at least sixty. That's an unscientific estimate based on my own observations. There were many widows, a few single men, and a number of couples. Students of traditional college age were conspicuously absent. Students under forty were rare.

What were all those old people doing eating sloppy English oatmeal and cold toast for breakfast in a medieval dining hall that resounded to the point of making most conversation impossible? What did they hope to accomplish by hoisting themselves out of ordinary dormitory beds to charge off to some classroom to hear lectures about literature, Renaissance art, prehistoric Britain, or the archeology of Oxfordshire?

They were keeping their curiosity alive—their heads turned on. Some were reviewing old facts; others were on their first trip to England and wanted a responsible overview of the country. Basically, these men and women were enriching their own lives, thereby remaining in the mainstream. In furthering their own interests, they would be of interest to others. When those oldsters talked about the "good old days," they probably meant 1066 A.D.

The shelves of every local library are loaded with books about the negative side of aging. Chronic diseases, financial planning, grief—all are covered by more authoritative sources than I could even pretend to be. The positive side of aging is what we are studying here. I agree with Richard Armour when he comments, "I hope I have a young outlook. Since I have an old everything else, this is my one chance of having a bit of youth as a part of me."

Having a young outlook is vastly different from looking young. On the shelves of any bookstore or library, during the commercials in any soap opera, in the pages of any magazine, we can all learn how to look young, or so the claims go. Looking young seems to be Priority Number One of Everywoman's World. I have never figured out exactly why. It would seem to me that any woman who likes herself at all likes herself at any age.

Although I cannot tell you how to take twenty years off your thighs, I can give you my never-fail rules for looking *older:*

1. Wear the same bright red lipstick that looked so good on you in the '40s.
2. Use enough dead-black hair color to give the impression you've been shampooing with Dyanshine.
3. Talk about your diet, your bad back, your teeth, your son-in-law, and your bladder at every opportunity.

The never-fail rule for feeling better about being older is maintaining a sense of humor. One charming *grande dame* in Colorado Springs claims she copes with her failing memory by feeling her toothbrush before she brushes her teeth. If it's wet, of course, she knows she's already done that.

What a young outlook she has! And what a joy she is to be around!

Family Life—
The Team Without the Coach

Revolving Doors—Family Life

"*I*t's okay with me if you want to move to New York, Mother. You don't need my permission, for God's sake. Just answer one question for me, though. Are you moving *from* something or *to* something? 'Cause if you're going two thousand miles to get away from the rest of us, we all have a problem."

That was number two son Ross, after I announced my intention of enrolling in Adirondack Community College for the fall semester of 1982. His concern was appreciated and exceedingly well stated, I thought. He was almost wrong in saying I didn't need his permission, however.

The subtle reversal of roles between my children and me had begun on the night of their father's death, although we did not recognize the fact until much later. For a while, we kept running into each other, getting in one another's way, in the revolving door between our old family structure and the new one we were all seeking.

These same convolutions occur with any change in family numbers—divorce, new marriages, more children. The trick is to come out of such upheavals with an improved working relationship among the survivors. Dependence has to be redefined. Exceptions are modified. Family life cannot go on in the same old way any more than any other drama can, once the cast of characters changes.

I certainly did not need permission to go east to college. What I *did* need was their approval, for my own peace of mind. The children became the review board for the parent. Women my age have made few, if any, major decisions on their own. Our parents expected obedience and acceptance of their plans for our lives. We consented without much fuss. Then our husbands took over the decision-making process in our traditional families. After all, they were the breadwinners. We expected to be second-in-command. Some of us have a really hard time trusting the momentous decisions we must make, now that we are on our own. We can learn. That's a top-priority project.

Family life needs a rebalancing for these later years. It's similar to changing strategies on the playing field. Somebody else is "it." That's an unfamiliar position for a mother from the '40s and '50s to play without the coach sending in new signals from the sidelines. I knew where I wanted the game to go, but I was unsure, at first, of my ability to call my own plays. It took practice, time, a few mistakes, and a lot of understanding. That adds up to a new maturity, of which I am mighty proud.

"Just leave Ross and Judy (or any of our offspring) alone about this," I used to yell at John. "They're adults. They deserve the chance to make their own decisions and live with their own mistakes." Looking back, I'm certain I sounded that tolerant and understanding when I agreed with what the younger-generation Weavers had in mind. I felt I had to get Good Old Dad off their backs, but I knew if matters really became traumatic Good Old Dad would rescue all of us.

Eventually, they came around to their father for the advice they needed. Nobody is reminding me to keep my nose out of the internal affairs of four Weaver households. I must do that myself. Every day. They are solid citizens, that family of mine, yet for some reason the urge to direct their lives seems even stronger now that I am a single parent.

Look at it this way: When John was alive, we had some heated discussions about our children and their growing-up problems. But we talked them over with each other more than we tried to argue with the youngsters involved. We aired our feelings about their crises with each other. Now I cannot do that, but I still have the urge to "talk things over," so I find myself bringing up subjects with my sons, daughter, and rarely with their spouses, that are absolutely none of my business. I just want to hear myself expound my great wisdom. That's bad.

My mother had the same problem. She was an active, alert woman who devoted every minute, every thought, of her adult life to her four daughters. She was first, last, and always a mother. We are, and always will be, her children. She had no real idea how old I am. My birth date was engraved on her memory, yet she still fussed about the shoes I wore, the cars I drove, the company I kept. Whenever I was about to appear in public to read from my work or make some sort of speech, she was a nervous wreck. She was my mother.

I used to remind her of my advanced age. It seems to me we should have been equals in the judgment department by that time and we found ourselves more and more in agreement. Sometimes, as a matter of fact, I'm convinced she was getting younger while I was getting older.

My feeble joke about all of her children being eligible for Medicare was not at all funny to my mother. I wonder why. Easy! Mother knew kids my age cannot even understand Medicare.

My sister moved into an elegant townhouse. Mother worried about her finding new friends in the neighborhood: "I don't know any young people who live there." When I suggested that my sister might ask around for a local chapter of AARP, Mother was not amused. Neither was my sister. So I suggested PTA. Worse.

This longevity business creates more four-generation families than ever before in our history. Perhaps some of us stay more alert and active in our sixties because we're still trying to prove to our mothers we can think for ourselves—which is what we are also trying to prove to our own children.

I'll tell you this much: Whenever I used to feel I'd been neglected by my own children or grandchildren, I'd rush to the phone to call my mother. Maybe I should have asked her for advice more often. She would have loved that.

*W*hat do I have the most of right now? Time. My time is my own to spend as I see fit. How can I best share this precious commodity with the most important people in my life—my family members—without taking too much of *their* time, without going into my Girl Scout-leader routine or laying on some sort of "after all, I *am* your mother!" guilt trip and running everyone's lives?

I heard a marvelous description of the pitfalls of this latter-day family planning during a writers' workshop at the Smithsonian: "My mother serves up guilt on a platter with the turkey at the family Thanksgiving dinner." Quite a lesson there. We want to spend time with our families, to be available when needed, without intruding on their own family life just as we hoped our own parents would do.

Forget the guilt part, the sense of obligation. If you and I have done so much for our children because they happen to be our children, we don't have to remind them how wonderful we are or how much they owe us. The pleasure we had being involved in the shaping of their lives is an adequate return. Whatever fun we have with them now is an unearned bonus. This can be the best time we've had with our own kids if we have sense enough to consider *their* feelings whenever some big idea hatches in our heads.

In his book *60 Plus,* Allan Fromme, psychologist, advises people with grown children to fill their lives so full of things to do and people to see they have no time for parenting. He's right, you know. We have so many opportunities and advantages around us, we have no business expecting our families to provide recreation and entertainment for senior citizens.

I have expanded Fromme's succinct advice into some reminders of my own. First, the don'ts:

Do not:

Drop in unannounced.

Insist upon family gatherings for all holidays.

Ask the same questions more than once a week.

Expect constant displays of gratitude.

Try to "buy" excess consideration.

Plan outings without consultation.

Offer advice unless specifically asked.

Insist upon paying all the dinner checks, or refuse to pay your share of the dinner checks.

Reminisce over and over again.

Contradict or interrupt habitually.

Turn down invitations, waiting for the family to call.

Say, "Your father always said . . ." or, "My father always said . . ."—that's worse.

This is a partial list. It boils down to being ourselves with an active life of our own instead of draping ourselves around our families' necks like some heavy old-fashioned cameo, to be cherished only for past glories, real or imagined. Never forget, nothing makes any of us seem older than conversation and activities centered on the good old days.

Here are the positive suggestions for Oma Weaver's Helpful Homilies for Family Harmony:

Do:

Make a concerted effort to find new topics of
   conversation with family members of all ages.
Concentrate on one-on-one experiences instead of group
   "command performances."
Be willing to travel to visit them instead of insisting
   everyone should "come home."
Reassure all family members of your availability and
   desire to help out in emergencies.
Demonstrate flexibility whenever you can.
Listen. Listen. Listen. Listen. Listen.
Plan outings with friends on Sunday afternoons.
Consult with parents before inviting some kid for a "treat"
   he might not enjoy.
Offer to run errands, help out, etc., only if both the spirit
   and the flesh are willing.
Stay alert for moments when the best thing you can do is
   disappear.
Add new interests to your own life without expecting
   family participation or enthusiasm.
Say "thank you" a lot.

*L*est I sound too Goody Two-Shoes for the reader, I hasten to add here that most of these do's and don'ts have been learned the hard way. During the past many years I have gotten along very well with my sons and daughter and their spouses most of the time. It would be foolishness to claim we always see eye-to-eye, or agree about my plans for my life or theirs. One of the worst mistakes of my entire life was interfering with opinions and advice in difficulties between one son and his wife and their teen-age boys. The pain I caused then was dreadful. It shall not happen again—a lesson not soon forgotten. Thank God for their tolerance of me during those days and their acceptance of me now.

One of our difficulties in dealing with the family problems of our children is the mistaken belief that such troubles are *our* problems at all. Also, we tend to look at the behavior of teen-agers in an outmoded way, forgetting the world has changed while we were busy getting old, or trying to stay young. B. F. Skinner's marvelous book, *Enjoy Old Age,* cautions us strongly about using outmoded standards for today's youth.

The same overworked ideas can get in the way of making a good time of leisure time with the family. Consider the grandmother who lovingly planned a wonderful family outing to cut Christmas trees in the woods. "We always had such a great time doing this when you were little. Remember? We picked out just which tree looked best and decorated it while it smelled so fresh and piney. Won't your children just *love* it? I'll bring the hot chocolate and the little sled. The one we always used. We'll leave really early on Saturday morning. Oh, Daddy would have loved this so!"

Saturday morning is bound to be a disaster, of course. One grandkid has a basketball game. A teen-age granddaughter has promised to go Christmas shopping with her friends. A perverse daughter-in-law cannot stand real trees because of the mess of needles on her new carpet. The dependable son calls to report trouble with the old reliable chain saw. And so it goes.

Two feet of old crusty snow covers the only remaining spot where cutting is allowed any more. The parking lot is two miles downhill. None of the kids wears boots. Mittens are wet. Noses are running. The real hot chocolate is not as good as the instant stuff at home. The cookies have been broken and the trees closest to the road have been partially consumed by pine-bark beetles. Three households have located only two decent trees.

Suddenly it's time to rush home because The Game starts at one o'clock on TV. The well-meaning grandmother drags her own wimpy little tree ("Oh, no, you take the fuller one. This is fine for me in my tiny place. I still have the ornaments you children made, so it'll be just fine for me . . . alone") into her living room and cries. Next week she'll complain to her bridge group about her ungrateful family who ruined the entire Christmas season for her.

That story reminds me of an old lady I knew years ago, back in Kansas. She said, "I don't care what they put on my gravestone as long as it doesn't say, 'She meant well.'" A sobering thought for our sixties.

*O*ne more point of sharing—as important as time to some of us— is money. The dilemma is relatively new. We have planned for our children to inherit our worldly goods when we die. If I live as long as the actuarial tables say I might, my children will be almost as old as I am now before they have the enjoyment or comfortable living that inheritance might provide.

Allison, my pragmatic daughter, stated the case plainly. "We don't expect you to leave us anything, Mother, but we would appreciate it if you'd come out even."

Mine is probably a purely maternal attitude, one not gleaned from authorities on financial planning, but this is the pattern of my lifestyle right now: After making certain my medical-care insurance is adequate and basic investments (mostly real estate and government mortgage whatevers) are secure for those coming days when I could be totally dependent on others, I will, by George, share all I want to with my youngsters now—while I can watch them enjoy it. And none of this making a scene about being fair. When my interest in this is equal, what I do for them will eventually come out even.

Several of the women I know feel this way. Others are still bound up in their belief that what was saved for our old age has to be sacrosanct until we die and we have an obligation to reinvest any earnings in order to leave even more for our children. We have only to watch any of the soaps—starting with *Dallas*—to see what happens when families argue about money. Those shows are popular because every family faces these problems to some extent. We, the widowed mothers or the wives of retired fathers, can work out some of those problems before one of our kids drags the others into court if we keep an open mind about the importance of money.

What on earth is this woman talking about? The next chapter will spell out how I have put my financial sharing with the family into effect. So far, I've had no complaints.

But the most important sharing is time and attention.

Always.

OMA AND HER BIG IDEAS

Dear Oma,

Thank you for inviting me!

I've been waiting to go to New York ever since I was an EMBRYO.

My mom says I will be there a week. See you in Wa. D. C.

Love, S. J. W.

*T*his letter from Sarah, written when she was eight years old, adorns the wall of my workroom—a constant reminder of the joys of grandmothering.

I was in residence in the Adirondacks. Ross and his family would be vacationing in Washington. I asked to join them for two days, then bring Sarah home to visit me before we both returned to Colorado for the summer.

Since my big move to Lake George part-time, I have made sure every one of my family has had a chance to inspect my home and lifestyle here in the East. It seemed important to me that they should be able to envision this life of mine away from them. Besides, I love this part of the country, which has been unfamiliar to them, and I want to share. One or two at a time have been here, including my mother and my sisters, of course. We have had some good times.

Intense planning has played a part here, particularly since the youngsters and I have a better time when we leave their parents at home. Flying to Albany is not that easy, so I arrange to meet the kids in New York, then proceed together to Lake George.

Here's how it worked once, in the spring of '84:

Two thirteen-year-old boys were involved. We carried out our rendezvous like the A-Team on assignment. I flew into La Guardia from Albany at ten o'clock. Whitney arrived from Houston at eleven. Jason's flight from Colorado came in at noon. We ate lunch at the airport, then took a two o'clock plane to Albany. My car was at the airport for the drive to Lake George.

For four days we played around in this area. Whit tried fishing, but no luck. Otherwise we "messed around" and they played basketball with a smurf ball in my living room.

Then we took Amtrak to New York City for two days. There we did it all: the Circle Line cruise, Empire State Building, a visit to the Stock Exchange, the Guinness Hall of Records, the Museum of Natural History, Hamburger Heaven, street vendors, *On Your Toes,* and dinner at Mama Leone's. And more. Those boys still had enough energy to play smurf-ball basketball in our hotel room. Then we did the airport routine in reverse.

That's what I mean by spending some of the money that could be put away for their parents to inherit in twenty years or for these kids to have, perhaps, when they are in their sixties. Who wants to go to Hamburger Heaven or play smurf basketball at the Waldorf Astoria when he's sixty?

My sons have been east for brief visits, which made little sense to them, I suppose. They took time from their work for a weekend Upstate. Now they understand when I refer to places they've seen or when I talk about the condominium. Most misunderstanding can come within a family by not knowing a situation first hand. If they want to disapprove, at least they can be logical about it.

𝓕 amily holidays are more relaxed than they were for a long time. We have had some memorable Thanksgiving dinners— memorable in a really negative way. Like the time one of my sisters' kids brought two dogs along for the family gathering and it snowed so hard we were all trapped inside and our dogs didn't like her dogs.

Or the time Chris dropped a root-beer fizzie in the turkey gravy.

Or some of the teen-agers sampled the bar.

Or the day when everyone invited seemed to have the impression I couldn't cook enough for such a crowd and showed up bearing bowls or pots of all sorts of stuff, demanding space in the oven or the overloaded refrigerator.

No more. Christmas is the same story. There used to be tension making all of the traditions work on Christmas Eve and Christmas Day. No more. Christmas-time in Beulah has been replaced by gathering in smaller groups wherever it's most convenient to get to church on time. The pomp and ceremony of ritual dining might work well in other families. We keep the whole affair simple, and enjoy each other and stray friends who drop by just at dinnertime.

Not all of our group projects or outings are expensive.

Miss Sarah and I had a fine time in Beulah when she spent the night with me. We fixed our supper in the wok and the bamboo steamer, dressed up in what passed for kimonos, and sat on the floor eating our Japanese feast and drinking tea from little cups. She was kind enough to help me up when it was time to do the dishes.

Sarah and I have also enjoyed our miniature golf games and the Colorado State Fair. In Colorado Springs, various kids and I have toured everything from the museum of the American Numismatic Association to the Olympic Training Center. We have flown kites and waded in streams. We have ridden old horses at a dude ranch and spent hours in the Metropolitan Museum of Art.

Nikki and I have driven from San Francisco to Pueblo, Colorado. My sisters and I found new fun being friends of old age when we drove from Colorado to New York together, sightseeing all the way.

Outfits like the Smithsonian offer travel plans that are learning experiences for any age. Those same two boys who played smurf basketball at the Waldorf Astoria were with me in the summer of '86 for an archeological dig in southwest Colorado. Allison, my daughter, came along. We had a marvelous time in lectures and lab sessions, and the boys enjoyed the week as much as did anyone in the crowd.

Their fresh sense of humor was a tonic for the rest of us, all older folks. Whitney and Jason entertained us by getting a spear caught in a tree outside the lodge with one mighty thrust of an atlatl, then heaving rocks at this huge cottonwood tree to dislodge the precious spear while the rest of us shouted encouragement.

Whit did confuse one "tenderfoot" nature lover by pointing out "rabbit berries," which he claimed came from "rabbit bushes." Oh, well. Allison and I were proud of our two teen-agers digging up more artifacts, sorting and cataloging them, than any other Smithsonian diggers.

There are hundreds of other opportunities for intergenerational vacation experiences like this. We're already looking for the next one.

*A*ll of this is a different kind of togetherness than we had before I became a widow. John and I spent time traveling and vacationing, but I would be a fool to think I can do exactly what we enjoyed, now that he isn't here. Not better, particularly, just different.

Two all-family excursions should be included here as suggestions for women uncertain about family travel. Once we went camping up near Aspen, as we had done when they were children. My sons and daughter and their families. I was highly complimented to be invited, and I loved every minute. The boys had brought along a special tent and cot for me—all the comforts to be afforded an old lady. We ate trout fresh from the lake for breakfast, hiked and waded, and had a grand time. That was special.

Then, instead of individual Christmas presents, I took those of the entire tribe who could get away to San Diego for a weekend. This was only possible because we are such a big family that the hotel gave us a group rate. That worked fine. We "broke up into smaller groups" for the most part—twenty-two of us including my sister and her family.

For this and for other outings in the future, the secret of success for all concerned is: don't suffocate each other. Some went to the zoo, some to Disneyland, some to see in-laws. We all went whale-watching on a three-masted schooner, but then again we did not cluster together like pigs at the trough. Each had his or her own fun.

Therein lies the secret of family activity when Grandma is the instigator: Give members of the group their own leisure time—their own space, as they say.

I hope I don't forget that part.

SISTERS

"*O*ur bond with our sisters is far stronger than our love for our husbands." Louisa May Alcott made that claim in *Little Women*. At least, Jo said that to Amy in the latest movie version of that favorite story from my childhood.

Terms like "sibling rivalry" and "birth order" had not been contrived by Dr. Spock and his cronies in our growing-up days. *Little Women* carries messages of mutual respect, loyalty, concern, accountability, and that old-fashioned bond of sympathy among family members. Happily, those qualities still linger in those of us old enough (I'm seventy now) to have grown up in the days of the "fictional" March girls: Meg, Jo, Beth, and Amy.

Ann, Middy, Mary, and I pictured ourselves as Little Women. The birth-order pattern of behavior in the book fit the four of us as closely as it enveloped the four Marches. How did Ms. Alcott know that much about birth order that long ago?

Little did we know or care at the time. I only realized that Ann acted like Meg, the oldest (sensible, always on the right side with our parents, dependable to the nth degree). I secretly thought of myself as Jo (adventurous, filled with imagination, all that good stuff). Middy was certainly Beth, third in line (eager to please and keep the peace, wanting to be an accepted member of the group, no matter what). Middy wrote notes to leave on Mother's pillow to avoid any possibility of confrontation when asking to go to the movies with the girls or have a picnic after school. Mary, whose full name was Mary Marn (after Mother), not only played the part of Amy the youngest to the hilt (demanding, petted, pampered, expecting the most of everything and everyone, yet enough talent and showmanship to get away with it), but expressed her ambitions well when only three or four years old: "When I grow up I'm going to be rich enough to wear silk housedresses."

Let's get back to that first quote about husbands and sisters, which may or may not be accurate. My cousin Barbara and I discussed the idea as we left the theater and *Little Women*. Barbara has two sisters and no brothers. Her baby sister Mary was referred to as "Little Blessed." Barbara had her doubts about sisters being more important in our lives than our husbands. Since that time I have found myself thinking a lot about my sisters and the way our lives are now.

Getting down to basics, consider this: Most of us knew our sisters long before we knew our husbands. Most sisters last longer in our lives than husbands do. Our sisters were a part of our formative years. They might understand our feelings better than our husbands. Sisters certainly see our point of view better than our children can.

After sifting all of this through my own head, I decided women our age ought to appreciate our sisters and pay more attention to them while we still have each other. Perhaps you and your sisters or brothers have managed to stay more concerned with each other than we Allison Girls have done. Since we really became friends after college, our separate families and separate obligations have interfered with sisterly "bonds."

Motherhood takes precedence. Our husbands expect our time and attention. I have heard some women say their husbands are actually jealous of time and attention paid to sisters. John was a little that way. Now—I'm speaking particularly to widows here—we have the chance to build an even stronger and more positive relationship with sisters.

For years our sisters were our competition. For the attention and favors of our parents, our teachers, the neighborhood kids, the boys, we pitted ourselves against each other without any overt declarations of war. Ann had more one hundreds in spelling. Mary Marn took tap-dancing lessons while I had to learn to play the piano. Middy weasled her way into learning to drive earlier than we did, and she wore lipstick to school.

The ultimate sibling rivalry/cooperation story, as far as I'm concerned, starred Mary Marn and me. The big interest in our lives focused under our grandmother's back porch. The cat and her litter of four kittens lived there. Each day we checked to see if their eyes had opened yet. Each one of us had our chosen kitten.

This was 1934, pre-penicillin days. My appendix ruptured. I was one sick little girl. Dad came home from the hospital realizing he had to prepare his other daughters for any eventuality—in those days, a ruptured appendix was generally fatal. After a tearful discussion of "Franny might die . . ." five-year-old Mary wiped her eyes and asked, "Who gets the other cat?"

Most of our lives, Ann and I shared a room. I resented her glorious red hair. Total strangers raved about Ann's hair. She would brush that red hair and put it up in pin curls while I watched, consumed with envy. Years later Ann told me how much *she* hated *my* hair because it was "crisp." My hair stayed in place; hers needed more of that gooey hair-set stuff you had to dip the comb in, remember? In one short conversation in our fifties, years of resentment were erased by one small admission of our girlhood feelings.

Perhaps we all need that. It has been said that carrying a resentment amounts to nothing more than allowing someone to live rent-free in your head. Once the old resentments of better grades, crisper hair, more shapely legs, or the ability to tap dance can be cleared from our heads, our sisters can still turn out to be the best friends we'll ever have.

Aside: What about older women who have no sisters, or whose sisters live far away, or still have husbands? Look around. A surrogate sister might be anywhere: on your block, behind you in church, or across the bridge table.

So what seems so special about sisterhood now, in our family? Remember, I write and speak only for myself. You might want to ask my sisters that question. You might get different answers.

For me, the revelation of what great traveling companions I have built-in came with my exodus from Colorado to Upstate New York to go to college. I mentioned this earlier in this book. Ann and Middy (recently widowed) drove cross-country with me, but we allowed ourselves ten days for the trip. Women driving together, we discovered, can stop at any root-beer stand, take any side road, linger over any cup of coffee or historical monument. No kids whining in the back seat, no man at the wheel refusing to ask directions or stop for Milky Ways or a restroom. Quite a change from our husbands, and certainly a departure from our father's travel pattern.

We admired the arch in St. Louis, the battlefield at Gettysburg, and the sights at Harpers Ferry. We dined with friends in Indianapolis and Carlisle, Pennsylvania. We got lost near Philadelphia when Ann drove; went the wrong way on a freeway ramp when I had the wheel. Middy's driving turn in midtown Manhattan made her nervous, but Ann and I helped her by keeping a cheerful positive attitude. She said we giggled.

Basically, we had a fine time.

Travel together, small suppers when we can visit without the grandkids, frequent but not incessant phone calls all add up to a respect for each other's individual obligations but closer family ties whenever. . . .

Our younger sister, Mary, divorced and just recently qualified for Medicare, has a great bed-and-breakfast place in Sedona, Arizona. Middy and I have stayed with her—as a matter of fact I helped her move from Scottsdale. I knew Mary's cooking could win prizes, but seven colanders? Financially, but more important, emotionally, Mary has needed and appreciated the support of her sisters in this new venture. My satisfaction in being able to help has exceeded the bounds of friendship. (Besides, she sells a lot of my books to her B&B guests.)

On my cruise/lecture trips, my sisters have been my guests. Since I live a more footloose life, my greatest chance to talk with my sisters one on one and share the ship and the trip provides all of us the time and freedom to know and appreciate each other during these years "of final options."

Other sisters? I have seen many at home and in my travels who obviously enjoy being sisters now more than ever before. I watch some and find out they still sing together (in a much lower key), share jokes together, compare books, art, plays, or crafts together, and often manage to fix old family favorites like "noodle pie" for a quiet evening together.

Middy and Ann still have husbands, whom I enjoy, but the sister part of our lives grows more important daily. Louisa May Alcott would approve of the Allison Sisters.

So would our parents!

AFTER ALL, I'M STILL YOUR MOTHER

*M*y mother hasn't had a new thought in fifteen years!" It could have been those words from one of my friends up in Beulah that prompted my intense interest in aging. Or aging and mothers. Or aging of our own.

So how can we cope with all of this aging business, especially in our own families? I used to think we could reduce the stages of our lives to the simplest of terms, like "taking turns." When I was born, it was my parents' turn to take care of me: bathe me, comfort me, change my diapers, and get me to eat the right foods. When my parents get to the other end of their time-line I should take my turn with them: bathing, feeding, changing diapers, and comforting.

Life is not that simple, is it? These days, our parents live much longer than their parents did. We find ourselves caught in what my friend Alice Uhl calls the Sandwich Generation. Our parents need, but don't necessarily want, our help. Our children have their own families, but working mothers leave grandmothers fuming about "Someone ought to spend more time with those children." There in the middle we find ourselves ready to retire to the gracious, peaceful life we had always pictured. There in the middle of the sandwich like a piece of bologna with people taking bites on all sides.

Sociologists, gerontologists, amateur and professional do-gooders have pontificated about this phenomenon. At the same time our outside world has undergone faster change than ever before. We haven't had as many old people before, and we've never had so many "advances" to keep up with at the same time—both of which can confuse and confound those of us classing ourselves as the older generation. We sound to each other like that old lady watching the parade: "Everybody's out of step but my boy."

A young man in San Diego called his old aunt—actually his great aunt—to invite her to a party. "Julie and I want you to come over on the 22nd for a family barbecue in our back yard. We have just redone the patio and the pool and it's terrific. We want our first party out there to be on the 22nd. For your birthday, Aunt Cora."

His aunt listened patiently to ravings about the new bushes and all that, then said quietly, "I appreciate being invited to your party. I'm sure your yard is splendid. It would be nice to see Julie and your family, but I cannot come to the barbecue. Have a good time. Thanks for asking."

The young man was devastated. "But this party is for you, for your birthday. All of the family will be here. It won't be a party without you. You are the guest of honor."

"Well, Johnny, I understand. But I will not be there."

"Why? Why won't you come to your own birthday party?"

"Because, Johnny, I can't merge."

"Merge? What's with this 'merge'?"

"Johnny, you have a nice new house and a fine back yard, but I cannot get there without driving on the freeway, and I can't merge. Those cars whiz by so fast they scare me. I get halfway up the ramp and I just freeze there. So I cannot come to your party and that is that!"

Hanging up the phone, and later recounting the conversation, John remarked, "I guess that's the way with a lot of us. We get so we can get halfway up the ramp but we can't merge. Most of life—not just freeways."

The message in that story comes in at least eight layers. Ironically, the outstanding message there for me has doubled up. I used to tell that tale about Johnny's aunt thinking of its implications in my mother's life. Before she died at ninety-two she had retreated more and more inside her own head. Merging with her outside world vanished from her capabilities. Now I think about and repeat that story with reference to myself and my own future, which necessarily means reference to my own children coping with my coming frailties of mind, body, and spirit.

Morbid? I don't think so. All of our lives we have seen older sisters, classmates, neighborhood pals, teachers, in-laws, even doctors, bankers, and bridge partners, as an example of what we will become. We spend our lives picking out good and bad specimens of "what I'll do when I'm that age."

With any luck at all, we improve on those examples.

As with any other condition to deal with, acceptance carries the key here, in coping with our oldsters and in anticipating our own problems. Acceptance of Mother's almost total lack of short-term memory proved difficult in our family. We would all say soothing words like "I'll see you next Tuesday," forgetting (ourselves!) that Mother wouldn't know in three minutes what we had said about next week.

To me, the most thoughtless remark we can make to an older person is, "I told you that yesterday." We must accept the fact those synapses no longer connect the wellspring to the reservoir. Nothing sticks. That's why my cousin Barbara claims to have a Teflon brain. Once we remind ourselves about memory loss, we can straighten out conversations with the old folks, not minding how many times they ask the same question.

Prime example: One day Mother had too much company at one time. Daughters and granddaughters all at once. One well-meaning granddaughter had even brought her dog to "visit Grammy." Mother was fit to be tied.

Ten minutes after the departure of all of those visitors, Mother complained to my son Chris. As far as she was concerned, she had been sitting there alone all day. To have reminded her of the other crowd would only have confused her.

My sisters and I should have accepted much more than Mother's short-term memory. Her needs seem so obvious now. For instance, Mother loved playing cards. She and Dad played cards a lot. Mother's bridge game and her general card sense could have helped her through those declining years if we had had nerve enough and sense enough and guidance enough to insist upon her moving to a pleasant, cheerful, caring environment where she could be playing cards (keeping her brain alive) far more often than her daughters could manage to spend time with her in her solitary refuge, which her home became.

Why did we allow this degeneration to happen? I don't even need hindsight to answer that question. Mother had always been in charge. "Don't upset your mother" had been the byword, even from our aunts. In that same little-girl submissive mode, we refused (all four of us) to parent our parent. She'd get mad and scream.

I wish I could remember the name of the doctor in Kansas City who told me about his mother and his sister. This man's sister lived in Topeka, their mother in Lawrence, Kansas—between her two children in the old family home crammed with all of her treasures. Mother would not move to the Presbyterian Home no matter what. Finally she fell, broke her hip, and lay for hours at the foot of the steps until the daughter arrived.

"That does it," proclaimed the son. The mother was furious, the sister livid. How could he not respect Mother's wishes about staying in her home with her things?

No matter. Old Mom was enrolled and ensconced in the Presbyterian Home screeching and wailing. The sister, ordered by her determined brother to stay absolutely away for three weeks, sulked, pouted, and called daily to ask about Mother.

After the prescribed three weeks, these people (both in their fifties) arrived at the Home. Their mother greeted them with even more venom than she had spewed when they had dragged her into the place. "How could you treat me that way?" the old girl cried. "How could you have kept your own mother cooped up in that gloomy old house when all of my friends have been out here having fun and playing bridge and going to shows in Kansas City?!"

Maybe the moral of that story is "You can't win." Maybe. More often it means we must follow our best instincts and hope we've done the right thing, just as we toilet-trained the toddlers and attempted to guide the teen-agers.

Have you noticed how many new professions and fields of expertise have suddenly appeared in our Yellow Pages and our Sunday supplements since the realization that old folks mean big business? Have you been reading about the new breed of social worker, the geriatric-care manager? For a price, we can hire a trained person, a stranger, to come into our homes and our lives to decide what to do about our old folks.

This could solve the dilemma for a great many families. After all, if I haven't tried it, I shouldn't knock it. The financial, emotional, and physical burden overwhelms our generation more than some of us realize.

No parent exists who has not said with varying degrees of frequency: "I don't want to be a burden to my children." At the same time, few and far between are the forty- and fifty-year-olds who have not moaned, "I don't know what we're going to do about Mother," or even worse, ". . . her/his mother."

No recitation of the possible ills or complications of our oldest years serves our purpose here. Why tell you what you already know? Every family differs in fundamental ways. Generalities abound from *Modern Maturity* to the Sunday supplements. The bleak side of family relationships has been exploited by every insurance company west of any given point. As my son Ross loves to say, "Let's get down to the rat-killin' here."

I am thoroughly convinced that communal living—life-care retirement facilities—offers the best choice for me. Notice I did not say for all of us. From here on I speak for myself and explain only myself. That's the way this book works—if it fits for you, so much the better, but I am not the Answer Man. I make this decision from observations of older folks, particularly Mother.

Sitting in her same chair, facing the same paintings, watching the same newscasts, reading the same Agatha Christie novels, eating the same dabs of food, waiting for services rendered by her number one daughter did absolutely nothing to prolong the quality of life Mother had enjoyed. We were happy she didn't get hooked on the soaps or enjoy a little nip now and then. Having no outside stimulation except lunch out once in a while seemed to me to shrivel Mother much faster than the women I watched in retirement communities.

"Mother needs something going on around her; even if it makes her mad it will at least get her circulation going," I thought every time I saw her. She had to have someone with her, but the women available for hire did not converse easily or play gin rummy, and soon found getting along with Mother too difficult to hang onto the job for long.

One year before she died, I watched with anguish as my son Ross carried his shrunken, helpless, semi-conscious grandmother into her home after yet another bout of pneumonia and a hospital stay. From there it had to be a full-time nursing facility.

In that place the personnel, trained and caring, made Mother's last year at least comfortable. In that place she found more than any of her daughters could have given her by trying to keep her "at home." I am convinced Mother understood that.

You get the picture. Now what will I do for myself and for my family? I fully intend to make the "life-care" move at seventy-five. Visualizing myself as still able to function, travel, and get around on my own, I will ease into the communal style of living before one of my sons or grandsons has to carry me into a nursing home to vegetate the rest of my life away.

With Mom (me) in a comfortable, congenial environment with people around to talk to (or not), meals to eat in the dining room (or not), nursing care when I need it (or not), bridge games or field trips to participate in (or not), my life will be well-enough filled to relieve my children of the frustrations, at least in my own mind.

Of course I have long-term-care insurance and all that. Even more important in my own mind, we have had down-to-earth conversations about this around the family table. Each of my children has in-laws to deal with, too—I have not forgotten that.

Facing eventualities with at least this much planning and acceptance of the fact that my turn is coming ought to smooth the way for all of us. That's the least I can do.

"AND HOW ABOUT THE TIME WE ALL . . . ?"

*W*hat keeps a family together—all on the same side? What transforms a family into friends, as well as people united by the coincidence of having the same ancestors (living in the same house, going through the same traumas of learning to roller skate, sharing algebra homework, fighting over whose turn to do the dishes)? In my opinion, families need a family sense of humor. The old "folks who laugh and play together can stand each other" theory.

My own growing-up family loved a good laugh. As kids, my sisters and I grew up hearing funny stories of our parents' childhoods. Grandmother lived across the street from us in a typical Victorian house with a sleeping porch. Grandmother told us regularly about how much our dad hated having to feed the chickens in the back yard. Dad and his sisters fought constantly about feeding those chickens.

One moonlit night a guy with a gunny sack crept into the chicken pen, causing something of a ruckus, stealing chickens. My Aunt Jim punched my dad, asleep in the next bed, so they both watched the chicken thief. Aunt Jim started to yell, but her nine-year-old brother clapped his hand over her mouth and shoved her back onto her bed. "Shut up, you fool!" he whispered. "Maybe he'll take 'em all." And he did.

My youngest sister, Mary, often managed to come up with some quip. One we all recall came one evening when our father (the consummate story-teller) regaled friends about his good times at a Republican convention. He borrowed a camera, put his hat on backwards, and pretended to be a press photographer. Without film or credentials, he claimed that self-important people posed like fools when he stuck out his hand and said, "I'm Allison from the *Times.*"

Little Mary, sitting beside Dad, stuck out her hand. "I'm Brown from the *Sun.*" After that, she had center stage in our gatherings.

The Weaver family had a different sense of humor—sometimes, in my opinion, almost cruel. The first "funny" story I heard from Joe Weaver (John's father) sent the whole family into hysterics over some poor klutz at the court house who had stapled his own finger to some papers. Joe loved telling about the man who thought his wife would look good in something long and flowing, so he dumped her in the Mississippi River. They made constant jokes about John's mother's singing, which really *was* awful, but she couldn't help that. Later, John's sense of humor mellowed some, and my favorite quotes after fifteen years of widowhood are often some funny remark of his.

Certainly other favorite quotes come from the children and the grandchildren. Jason, our first grandson, spent the most time with us, and kept us entertained on a regular basis. Jason and I picked wild plums and I made jelly that didn't quite jell as Jason and I had pictured. With our plum jelly dripping off his toast, Jason said, "Oma, next time you make this delicious jelly, can I just drink it?" I'll never look at a jar of jelly again without seeing that small round face with the big blue eyes asking that question, even though it happened twenty years ago.

Jason really had a way with words—still does. Shortly after the jelly episode we had a picnic in the rain on a mountainside. His attitude was about the same: "Oma, next time you say 'Jason, do you want to go on a picnic?' I hope I say 'No.'"

Obviously Jason's ability to succinctly state his feelings about such matters comes from his mother. About a month before Jason was born, I remarked to very pregnant Judy, "Tomorrow I plan to go to Denver for a meeting."

"What kind of a meeting?"

"Judy, I'm going to a meeting of the Colonial Dames." I said that with some pride, as I recall.

"What sort of a meeting is that?"

I probably took a deep breath. "Judy, the Colonial Dames are what is known as an ancestral society. As a matter of fact, when your baby is born, he will be a thirteenth-generation American."

(I cannot hear a lot of humility here, can you?)

Judy looked down at her bulging midsection and grinned. "Oh. And he's SO excited about it!"

I needed that. Those words haunt me whenever my own superiority and importance loom larger than life.

Jason's cousin Whitney is a Texan, the only son of my only daughter. When Whit was three, he, his mom, John, and I were in The Galleria in Houston. A wonderful kite shop held the attention of this bright-eyed boy and his grandmother. John turned thumbs down on a visit to that kite store, which dismayed Whit for a minute or two. Then he brightened. "I have a good idea," he crowed, looking at his mother, grandfather, and me. "Let's break up in smaller groups."

Absolutely my favorite story comes from one of my mother's visits with me in my new single life at Lake George, New York, while I was in that second college career. Whole-hearted approval of my changed lifestyle seemed impossible for Mother—I could just as well have stayed at home, in her opinion. Little "digs" filled her conversation.

"Aren't you going to lock your door?" Mother asked in that don't-you-know-any-better voice she had used for sixty years beginning with "Pick up your socks."

I replied in my I'm-a-big-girl-now voice I'd been practicing for fifty years. "No, Mother. We're only going to walk down to the docks. We won't be out of sight of my front door and there are plenty of neighbors around."

Mother huffed. A sound I knew very well. For all of those years Mother's huffs had put me on the defensive.

As usual I tried to justify my position here. Exactly like explaining why I forgot my leggings in the cloakroom at school or failed to practice my piano lesson. "Mother—" (even to myself I sounded like a pleading child) "this place is safe. Besides, I'm sixty years old and I've never been robbed yet."

After one more huff, Mother said, "Well. That doesn't say much for your stuff, does it?"

Once or twice this new lifestyle has been less than perfect. Having a sense of humor made a big difference in one really disappointing speaking trip. The gigantic "Senior Festival" advertised never happened. That is, nobody came. Not one ticket was sold. Exhibitors including hearing-aid people, health-food merchants, musicians, refreshment-stand operators, a couple more writers—we all showed up for two days in Spokane at the Fair Grounds, by ourselves. After the first few hours, the promoter disappeared.

What does one do in such circumstances? First of all, this did not appear to be a life-threatening turn of events. Just in case someone showed up to test our hearing aids, buy our vitamins, rent our wheelchairs, or buy our books, we stayed.

We entertained ourselves. The musician thumped out "When You Wore a Tulip" and the herbal remedy lady sang. The hearing-aid man interviewed the massage guy standing on the wobbly platform with a makeshift sound system. I told jokes and the assistant to the long-gone promoter/director gave away tiny cups of Smuckers sherbet. We all ate as many hot dogs as we could hold. We exchanged samples, brochures, and books. Most of all, we laughed.

"Where have you had the best audience?" I am sometimes asked. The answer is a toss-up between Spokane and the Mount McGregor Medium Security Correctional Facility upstate in New York, but that story takes even longer to tell.

The ability to see the less-serious side of life in any set of circumstances pays off in cutting the stress level. We all know that. Instances like this Spokane adventure help, however, in focusing the importance of an outlook that adds the balance of humor when the best-laid plans slide off the deep end.

Closest to home and to the heart are family jokes and humor, of course, most of which surface when triggered by similar experiences or have become a part of our family verbal shorthand. This connection of the mutual understanding of special words keeps the relationship unique to us. That bolsters spirits in time of crisis, or softens anger or pain with reminders of shared experiences even in the most serious of circumstances.

Most of us consider an inside joke in the family to be part of our precious heritage even more valuable than Aunt Emma's Spode tea set. At least that sentiment exists in my family and its value becomes more apparent every day.

Mother died. Just recently, after more than ninety-two years and one year in a nursing home, Mother gave in to the forces of aging that had been eating at her bit by bit. Our family had been close around in those last days. Mother had had the best of care. We could have no regrets that she no longer would feel the helplessness and futility of a life she no longer considered useful—or even pleasant.

In other words, we could not mourn for Mother; our sadness, our sense of loss, was for ourselves. Her four daughters, her thirteen grandchildren and their spouses, uncounted great grandchildren gathered to celebrate her life among us, to recall the best of our moments with her. We also gathered to reassure each other that our family remains intact. This matriarchal mother of ours outlived the rest of her generation by years. Her death marked for us the termination of an entire generation of aunts, uncles, our father, even their close friends whom we called "Aunt" and "Uncle."

Now we, my sisters and I, are that generation in our own families. We're the old folks.

Mother's favorite minister of her church carefully and lovingly recalled Mother and her special ways for all of us during one of the gentlest, most thoughtful services I have experienced. In recounting some stories of Mother and the family, he brought laughter to the crowd, laughter appreciative of family attitudes and close relationships. Mother would have loved that.

Mother would have loved even more the gathering of her brood later in the day. My sister's home filled to bursting with the clan—all visiting, all eating, all recalling happy days of childhood and times shared. Yet each of us was aware that this probably will not happen again—all of us gathered under one roof at one time. Grammy was the catalyst bringing all of us together for this last time. Each family now grows in its own direction.

One special part of that family gathering struck home. One of our nieces had brought along a video of Mother's eighty-seventh birthday party. In the midst of all of the telling and retelling of our marvelous family jokes resounding all over the house, she insisted upon viewing this five-year-old video.

Personally, I thought that was a dumb idea. The day was going well. Why gum up the works with a stupid video? Morbid.

Boy, was I wrong. On that video from 1987 there we all were. And we were telling the same jokes that had just consoled us on this day in 1993. Do you hear what I'm saying? Not only does our family tell the same stuff over and over for years on end; that same stuff assures the continuity, the closeness, the wonder of being a family. Family humor. Blest be the tie . . .

Friends—
A Whole New Ball Game

A WORLD FILLED WITH OLD WOMEN

*B*efore you turn another page in this book I want you to stop for a minute—no more—and write the first five words that come into your head when you think, "old woman."

Right now. Jot the words here on the margin or on the flyleaf, or on the back of the nearest envelope next to that list you forgot to take to the market yesterday. Do not cheat by reading on. "Do not pass GO. Do not collect $200." Stop here and write five words, honest words. First-impression words. What do you think of when someone says, "old woman"?

I'll be fair about this. I'll reveal the list I wrote when I first confronted this challenge during a writers' conference two or three years ago. I wrote

bad breath
poor posture
lonely
whining
irritating

Others in the group added glowing adjectives like

> *boring*
> *repetitious*
> *self-centered*
> *old-fashioned*
> *poor*

From that exercise I learned two instant lessons:

I have been an unreasonable snob about older women.

I do not want to be any of the above.

The wise woman conducting the seminar was not surprised by our answers. She then directed us to write five *positive* words about old ladies. That took all of us a lot longer. My list was something like this:

> *personal freedom*
> *leisure time*
> *chance to learn*
> *extra buying power*
> *good health*

This is one of those workshop experiences that refuse to be packed away in the bottom drawer, never to be seen again. These lists of five haunted me because they were about *me*. Only *I* could do anything about those negative and positive images. Nobody else. It had to be me.

The best way to attack any general problem is to reduce the question to specifics.

When had I formed those negative images?

Were they all from my childhood?

Who were the old ladies with the bad breath and the poor posture?

What older woman had been so irritating that I'd even thought of that word?

As a kid and as a young woman I was constantly aware of denture breath, coffee breath, and smokers' breath. The principal reason I never smoked was the awful odor of smokers who insisted on whispering in my face. My parents' friends, aunts, or older cousins would hug me and their breath was terrible. I resented the unpleasant aura around them almost as much as I did the inevitable remarks about how big I was for my age and the comments about how girls "these days" wear their dresses too short or "have no sense about comfortable shoes with good arch support."

The first individual to come to mind from my adult experience was a not-so-old woman on a small-ship cruise of the Scandinavian Waterways. She was a retired professional woman of some sort. Her complaints about the food, the crew, the itinerary were loud and incessant.

Worse than that was her appearance. In six days, she did not comb her hair or change her dress. When the Swedish stewardesses offered to help her shower or clean herself up, she refused, saying, "I don't have to look at me. These other people do. I'll never see them again."

She was surely right about that.

Then there was a standout passenger on another cruise who ordered fish for dinner on the second night out. Much to her surprise, since she had not asked about terms on the menu, the fish was covered with a hot Spanish-style sauce. One bite burned her mouth.

The waiter hurriedly replaced the dinner, but that woman spent the rest of the cruise talking about her digestion and "the way they cook fish on this boat." To this day, if she's asked about her Alaskan cruise, her answer will not be a description of Russian dancers in Sitka or the museum in Juneau. You'll hear about that damnable fish sauce—if you're foolish enough to inquire at all.

On that same cruise was a dear lady, Mary Whelan. Mary should have posed for Norman Rockwell. Her smile was infectious, her laughter appealing. Anything that might have displeased her she treated as her own problem. Mary was a great favorite with our fellow passengers. Even though she was only eighty-four at the time—tiny, huggable, always wearing a sassy little hat of some sort—whenever anyone asked her age, she'd say, matter-of-factly, "A hundred." And that was that. The contrast between these two women was memorable, obviously.

There have been admirable older women in all of our lives. Recalling them and their particularly attractive characteristics seems to me to be a worthwhile exercise for shaping my next twenty years.

Mae Reed Porter lived in Kansas City when John was an intern and resident there. I saw her rarely, but each time was a real occasion for me. I'm certain she would never remember me at all from the few times we chatted during Pi Phi alumnae meetings. Mrs. Porter was tall, erect, not quite graceful. Her white hair was short, her face lined but pleasant.

Mrs. Porter had traveled extensively by the time I knew her. In Baltimore, in the back room of a bookstore, Mae Reed Porter had found stuffed into a cereal box some early-day prints of a Scottish hunting party in the American West. Fascinated, Mrs. Porter set out in search of the identity of the hunters and the history of their expedition. From that cereal-box beginning, she wound up writing *Across the Wide Missouri* with Bernard DeVoto.

This great lady wore bright tartan capes. She was a presence wherever she was. Her mind was much quicker and more fertile than were those of us less than half her age. Yet, her travels and her writing were not necessary for her livelihood. Mrs. Porter could have joined the rest of her social set for lunch every Wednesday and cocktails regularly at the Mission Hills Country Club. Instead, she was off to Greece or sequestered in some library, finding out more about the world that so fascinated her, and vice versa.

Florence Means never wrote any widely known books, but she will always be one of my role models. Florence was also tall—an imposing figure of a woman in any setting. (Is this one reason I am so distressed about shrinking to five foot eight in my old age?)

Florence's outlook never aged. She never shrank, at least in my eyes. She wore fine big hats and told funny stories about living on a sheep ranch or learning to fly a plane in her sixties. Nothing seemed to have happened in her world—near or far—that failed to interest Florence.

Thinking back, that was her charm: She was always interested.

Lillian Morrison lived well into her nineties and her eyesight failed, but she never lost her zest for living or her ability to keep up with the world around her. I was in charge of a group cruise, a fundraiser, on board the *Delta Queen* in 1973. It worried me to have a ninety-year-old passenger. On the first night out of Memphis, when I spotted Lillian Morrison perched on a bar stool, wine glass in one hand, song sheet in the other, surrounded by younger people straining to hear what she had to say, I knew we were in business.

My own mother was remarkable, even though she had a tendency to resist any sort of change, like wearing pantyhose or taking calcium. She lived alone until ninety-one, drove her own car, and managed her affairs far better than I. The inevitable difference in my feelings about her in contrast to other old women is not unusual: I just used to wish she'd stop mothering me.

If she had let up on being my mother, she would have been one of my best friends. In the past years, since I was writing about older women and we had been talking a lot about aging problems, my mother became much broader in her outlook, more tolerant of younger generations—and she lived in the midst of three layers of family. She almost stopped aging; she became younger. For that I am grateful as a lesson in my own dealings with my grown children and their families.

These are wonderful women. Writing about them brings tears to my eyes. When I read this chapter aloud to my number three son, I started to cry over Mary Whelan.

This remembrance does more, however. It reinforces my determination to seek out the admirable, the worth-knowing, older women in my world and make a conscious effort to be that kind of an oldster myself—friends of mine like Grace Callahan, who heads up a writing group in Leisure World; Fran Bayless, who never let a small irritation like a broken hip get her down; Mavis Todd, who swims every day and happily shares her expertise about foundations and grants and worthy causes.

Did you ever hear anyone say about an old woman, "She hasn't changed a bit in fifty years"? That's no compliment. Beware.

Change is essential in every aspect of our lives, particularly in our social lives, which we need to consider here.

OUT OF THE FRYING PAN . . .

"*H*ello. I'm Frances Weaver, a recycled housewife from Pueblo, Colorado."

Most of my speeches begin with those words. Four years ago, I guess, it occurred to me to say this to every audience. At first I thought it was clever—a snappy opening to give those folks out there the impression they were about to hear a light-hearted witty person talking about aging. Most of them didn't even want to think about that subject.

This has worked for me. I am by no means a nationally known figure. The audience, except for the few who had read my books or seen me on PBS, had only the introduction from their program chairman to go on. These people needed reassurance right off the bat. No diatribe about the need for increases in Medicare or the dangers of eating red meat would engulf them. Only a recycled housewife from Colorado, boasting no graduate degrees in gerontology, wearing little make-up, hair graying unevenly, clad in ladylike clothes and comfortable shoes stood at the podium.

Gradually it dawned on me exactly what I was saying. I had chosen "recycled" in place of "retread" from earlier speeches. Principally, changing terms seemed an update of language. Nobody talks about retreads any more. Recycle says more. Recycle tells my story: *There's more to me than I've used yet.*

Discussing our current approach to trash, a friend pointed out, "Labels are burned off the bottles in the beginning of the process." My mind wandered, no doubt, with the realization that I, and millions like me, have burned off earlier labels in refocusing ourselves into these marvelously productive and interesting years since we finished our first half-century. The analogy inevitably rolls on: Recycling ourselves means getting rid of whatever serves no useful purpose, whatever our lives no longer depend on. Recycling also means discovering the unused, still-new interests, options, and opportunities that did not fit the younger version of ourselves.

That's the best lesson learned in these past seven years since this book and I hit the road to spread our message: Recycling depends upon those same requisites necessary for any positive change in our lives, an open mind and willingness to try something new—to depart from our well-worn paths into new territory.

We recycle leftovers all the time. Years ago if we hadn't found a way to combine a few scraps of chicken with some leftover noodles and such, good food would have sat in the refrigerator in a plastic bag until moldy. Picture that. The last thing I want to see myself doing is sitting in a corner covered with green fuzz.

My recycling began almost twenty years ago, before the death of my husband. You have read that part in this book. The length and breadth—the scope of my recycled life—astonishes me and delights my family. More than anything, these years have been a continual learning experience. I have learned about people, places, and things totally unexpected in my younger, less flexible, more structured years. Sharing these experiences has become my greatest pleasure.

Learning what? The importance of choice, to begin with. In dealing with my own options as well as with my family, I realize more than ever the importance of accepting the results of our own choices. This lesson caught up with me late in life, but not too late. Too often we tend to blame anyone from the weatherman to the airlines to the trust department for the predicaments brought about by our own choices. Now if I choose it and it doesn't work, I can generally see how I chose the wrong action or the mistaken words. I don't necessarily broadcast such negative information, but I try not to ruffle a lot of feathers or carry a misplaced grudge.

Choice, in its positive sense, comes harder to all older folks, not only older women. A prime obvious example we can see is those hard-shelled whiners who insist on staying alone in their Family Home when they and that home no longer need each other. They complain to the rest of us about their trials and tribulations: clogged drains, rusty pipes, dying grass, unpulled weeds, accumulating trash, poor insulation, and the cost of getting someone to shovel snow. Travel? Oh my, no. They must stay at home to guard all of those treasures that someday the children are sure to cherish.

Do these groaners want our advice? Not really. Any of our suggestions will prompt a dozen or more reasons not to move. Those recitals of woes of possessions serve some mysterious purpose, probably dating back to their childhood or the Great Depression. (Or both.)

But here's one more important fact for older folks I have learned since I have been around the country giving speeches in retirement centers. In more and more communities these days, affordable, attractive, downright splendid housing-plus-care-plus-companionship-plus-security can be found—a far cry from the "Old Folks' Homes" of our youth. These retirement communities have grown to a big business. Competition means better services, more complete health care and assisted-living facilities, and more spacious and elegant surroundings. See for yourself.

Trusting our own decisions takes some time. Looking back, I can say going back to college, writing a column instead of trying for a best-selling novel, making lots of speeches for not a lot of money, trimming my living arrangements down to one quite-ordinary town house with no plants and no pets has worked for me.

Some have not been the best choices, like the convertible I loved and wrecked, the times I have involved my married children in ill-contrived adventures, the very few speaking engagements that turned out to be disastrous (but I chose to go!). All in all, my choices have not made any money, but the profits are enormous.

Making choices implies an acceptance of risk. Now, risk might be only a four-letter word, but it breeds fear and trembling in the hearts of many oldsters. They define risk as bungee-jumping or white-water rafting. I prefer risk to mean any venture outside our accustomed pattern. The "Ain't tried it, don't knock it" approach. My favorite question is "Why not?"

Every morning we should each make one primary decision in front of the mirror: "Today will I be the statue or the bird?" For those of us over sixty, three statue days in a row mean bad trouble. Without intending to, we can wither into the ingrown, gripey, self-centered, dull, forlorn, whimpering old coot with bad breath and a backache everyone expects us to become. Risk can mean little more than trying a new restaurant or taking a class at the local art museum, but risk pays off in new adventure, friends, and excitement.

One risk often leads to greater discoveries of our own capabilities. When we lived in Beulah, Colorado, in the mountains, every hike or ride led to canyons or meadows or streams unseen from our houses. I often think of those wonders of our little mountain town when one gate seems to open after another for me. Example? First, self-publishing this book was a risk that most of my friends thought foolish, I'm sure. After all, I could have stayed at home playing bridge and going to meetings. Why did I need to publish a book?

Shortly after *Grandmother Faces* appeared on the shelves of the Tattered Cover in Denver, a call came from a fine publisher in Golden, Colorado, wanting to buy the book to publish themselves. I refused because they wanted to make changes I could not accept. "I'll sell you one of my kids, maybe," I said, "but not that book." Consequently Fulcrum asked me to write a travel book for them to publish—*This Year I Plan to Go Elsewhere.*

The fun had just barely started there, folks. From that little travel book for older single women, I was invited to be interviewed by Arthur Frommer on a nationwide cable channel. (He publishes Frommer's travel guides.) I was also invited by the department of tourism in Malta (!) for a week in Malta complete with hotel, guide, car, and all sorts of great things. Now I know Malta. Now I love Malta. Now I suggest to all of you that Malta cannot be beat for a place to trace the progress of Western Civilization with minimal travel and maximum pleasure.

That *Elsewhere* book came out about six years ago. Two months ago I met a young woman at a conference about travel writing in California. "Why is your name so familiar to me?" she asked continually.

"I've seen your face someplace. But I have been living in Europe for four years. I just returned last week." After much speculation about her confusion, like maybe she had a friend of the same name, she remembered. "I just came from Malta. My guide there was an archeologist, a young woman. Said she had been your guide, showed me your book, and told me when I get back to the States I should tell you hello when I see you. And here you are." One more entry under "Small World."

Also connected with this book: my "job" as lecturer on the *Crystal Harmony,* a fine cruise ship of which I am so proud you'd think I built the thing and taught the captain how to sail her.

Back in 1988 a woman whom I did not know, Harriet Johnson of Bella Vista, Arkansas, heard a review of *Grandmother Faces* in her P.E.O. meeting. (My old Kansas City friend, Betty Holt, presented the book review that day.) Harriet telephoned her son Peter in San Francisco where he worked for Royal Viking Lines in the department in charge of enrichment lecturers. Harriet instructed her son—as every mother loves to do—to hire the author of that book for speeches on his ship. Well, I had already (two days before) talked to this dear young man about just that. He might have been mildly interested, but the call from Mother was all he needed. All I needed, too.

Some might call that luck. I call it synchronicity, and it can happen more than we appreciate or understand unless we have the old antennae out for such minor miracles. All of the threads came together that day. Pete did hire me for Royal Viking, which I enjoyed. Then we both switched to Crystal Cruises, a move I've never regretted. Since my sailing days began, I have met Harriet Johnson. She's a very nice lady, to whom I shall forever be grateful. Because of her P.E.O. meeting and that phone call, I have traveled to exotic places I never could have afforded, met all sorts of people, seen sights I never dreamed of, and been able to share these experiences with friends and my sisters. Literally hundreds of such examples fill my life story of the past ten years or so. I could write another book called *Isn't This a Small World?* but even coincidences become a bore after the first few pages. Suffice it to say one seemingly small event after another changed my outlook and re-created my life.

My dear friend Skippy who had married at seventy-two, supremely happy, said to me one day, "Honey, you're lookin' at Cinderella." I knew just how she felt.

WHO NEEDS A RIDE TO THE PARTY?

*T*his chapter has had as many false starts as an eight-and-under swim meet. Only the chapter about sex gave me so much to rethink when I read the first draft aloud.

Today the problem of writing about our social lives as singles in our sixties and seventies is clear and simple. I have come to the conclusion it's a matter of definition.

According to *The Concise Oxford Dictionary,* "sociable" means "ready and willing to converse, communicative, liking company, marked by friendliness, not stiff or formal." Therefore, "social" means "not fitted for or practicing solitary life, interdependent, cooperative."

Roget's Thesaurus suggests synonyms for "society": "friendship, companionship, intimacy, fellow-feeling, neighborliness, companionability, cordiality."

I asked my good friend Terry to describe her social life. She said, "Nil."

Terry's been a widow almost as long as I have, fifteen years or so. We are long-time friends. We've traveled together. She plays bridge every Monday with my sister. She plays golf most of the rest of the time. Terry is an attractive, bright, energetic, conservative lady. But she says her social life is nil.

Terry's definition of "social" is "party." So was mine, until I really gave the matter some thought. While looking up the words "social" and "society" in half a dozen reference books, I never once found the term "party" or "date."

Maybe our lives ought to be defined as "redefinition." During our entire lives we ought to reevaluate what we do. Social life meant "party" for most of us for years, but those parties changed as we aged. (It's important to use that word "aged." We have been aging since we were born. Aging did not suddenly invade our lives at fifty-five.) Birthday parties and school Valentine parties were replaced by teen-age parties in back yards, thence to college beer-busts out in the woods or dances at the sorority house. On to charity balls and the country club in our young-married phase, then we concentrated for years on at-home entertaining for couples, with a few widows thrown in as time went by.

Now the time has come for another transition in our social thinking. It's just that simple.

B. F. Skinner in _Enjoy Old Age_ puts it this way: "There is only one solution: escape from the control exercised by the fun you once had. . . . Limit yourself to the kinds of things you enjoy _as you are now._"

I would change the word "limit" to "treat" in that quote because we are all capable of having a good time if we put forth just a little thought and effort. But the entertainment is different from past years, and the effort must be our own.

This thought just came to me, illustrating what I'm saying: Back in my college days, we danced at a marvelous place, the Avalon Ballroom, which had a dance floor on springs. That's right, there were big springs under the wooden floor. When the place was filled, the whole ballroom bounced with the band. That was the greatest fun I could imagine at that time (although my sister claims it ruined my husband's dancing because ever afterward he just stood in one spot and bounced on *any* dance floor).

If I were foolish enough to return to the Avalon Ballroom in downtown Aggieville in Manhattan, Kansas, today, I'd break a hip before the band finished "One O'Clock Jump." Times have changed and so have we, girls.

Two old men met outside a supermarket in Florida. One was carrying a sack of groceries. "What did you buy?"

"Oh, just some bread and cheese and a head of lettuce."

"Why'd you buy it all at once? You could have made three trips."

See? Even an errand to the market can be a social event, or three.

Skinner, again, writes of an older woman who buys only enough groceries for one day. She forces herself to go out again tomorrow.

More often than not, we'll see someone we know in the store, someone who might like to come over for a cup of coffee one day. Someone who might enjoy going to a band concert or a ride to the country to find some really fresh corn.

Walking is another social event, a chance to get out among 'em and maintain your health and your image at the same time. If the people who walk at eight don't interest you, walk at nine, and so on. If one route is a bore, go another direction. Change.

Being too tired or too lonely to get out of the house is not the *reason* to stay in, it's the *result*. Boredom is ninety-nine per cent self-inflicted. That's what this book is all about.

Spur-of-the-moment entertainment is possible for us, now that we don't have to be at home to put the roast in or start the potatoes, pick up kids here, deliver them there, be on hand (with a drop of O'Cedar behind each ear) when our lord and master walks through the kitchen door expecting a feast suitable for the Prodigal Son on any day ending in *y*. We have our own time to make our own fun, to be "communicative, liking company."

Spur-of-the-moment works. Next time you are standing at your kitchen sink, staring into space, feeling left out, ask one question: "What would I really like to be doing right now? Or tomorrow? Or this weekend?"

Unless your answer is "making love," with which I cannot help you, head straight for the phone. Do not wait 'til morning. Do not stop to analyze who asked whoever the last time. Call someone who is likely to be in the same frame of mind and suggest anything plausible, just to get out.

Or invite someone in. Right now. I do a lot of entertaining. By that I confess I'm entertaining *me* as much as my guests. Some of my best little evenings have been launched by an extra piece of chicken. This is an age-change we can easily overlook. In pick-up excursions or last-minute get-togethers, I am entertaining myself and my friends. If they have a good time, swell. If I have a good time, that's even better.

This new slant on sociability—for most of us—whenever and wherever, without written invitations or complicated arrangements, wipes out the tendency to stick to the who-owes-whom pattern that has hamstrung so many older women. Exploring new territory, eating different food, studying the work of favorite artists (or of unknowns), listening to readings in the local library, or going off to a jazz festival or chamber music in a barn improves the quality of our lives.

Expanding horizons and laying groundwork for new friendships and activities make life more interesting. Sulking in front of *CBS News* cannot do that.

*B*ack to the title of this chapter, "Who Needs a Ride to the Party?" During my career as the greatest hostess west of any given point, I never failed to plan one big party during the summer when I invited all of our widowed friends. I'll bet you've done that, too. This was a ritual. The single women arrived together, generally sat together, and left together, but I was satisfied that I had entertained the poor old souls. They were convinced my parties were better than eating corn flakes at home alone.

I did not understand, until widowhood engulfed me, that those women would have had a much better evening one or two at a time in smaller groups. I expected them to appreciate sitting like birds on a wire while the couples of the crowd stopped along to chat, often to say how much they missed "good old Hank," or reminisce about "Dave's smiling face" at these gala events. To the widows they usually said, "How are you getting along these days?" To which the widows answered, "Fine, thanks, but . . ." And that was that.

Any single men at the party concentrated on the married women, for a number of reasons too exasperating to mention.

There is no reason on earth for me to expect my still-married friends to be more concerned or wiser about widows at parties than I have been. They'll find out soon enough for themselves. The same is probably true of your hostess days. We are not trained to be socially adept single women. That's a new skill for us to acquire, a challenge we must not ignore.

We can all see, when we are willing to admit it, that we do not belong in the coupled world any longer. Not in the sense of husbands and wives in the social setting that conventionally centers around even numbers. Four in a car is fine. Five is uncomfortable in today's cramped back seats, and so forth.

Aside from such complications, however, consider this: We widows remind men in their sixties of their own vulnerability, their own perishability. We are living messages to our women friends that they will almost certainly be in the same boat, one of these days.

Some married women seem to think of any single woman at the party as a threat to their own marriages. That says something about their shaky marriages, but more about their self-esteem. Being a widow is not the worst thing that can happen to a woman. Most men don't want to know that. Many of their wives just don't want to think about it at a dinner party or, worse still, a weekend in the country.

Some married women have a tendency to glare at me across their buffet plate of Mexican chicken and tossed salad when I admit I have just returned from a trip to Paris for lunch (an exaggeration, of course) while they have been watching their husbands fly-fishing for the thirtieth summer in a row. Or they are still spending weekends watching good old Charlie sleep in front of TV after he finishes cleaning the garage on Saturday afternoon.

Such thoughts fill these women with guilt feelings. Better they should get the message I should have heeded in my own marriage and say, "Charlie, the garage can wait. We're gonna go watch the whitewater races on the river this afternoon," or some such.

Charlie deserves more credit than he gets, sometimes. But for now, neither husbands nor wives relish the company of a free-wheeling widow whose world is wide open and independent of men, chatting happily in front of their spouses. "Widows are such a bore. Why can't they just stay home like the rest of us?" some women will say, but the edge of envy in the voice is hard to disguise.

his brings up our obligation as widows to be thoughtful guests. Here is my guest list of *do's*:

Contribute to the conversation without dominating.

Be alert to opportunities to be helpful without being in the way or suggesting "better ways."

Check with your hostess about her well-laid plans before arriving at the front door laden with your marvelous home-made cheese puffs or your favorite wine.

Talk sports with the men, diets with the women, and grandkids with everyone.

Offer on weekends to sit on the floor and play cards with small children, if necessary.

One *don't* is enough:

Do not mope around or talk about the good old days unless someone else brings up the subject. Then smile a lot.

So who needs a ride to the party? You don't. Neither do I.

New Contacts, New Skills

*T*his is where the excitement really starts. Out there waiting for us is a wide world we have never explored. Oh, we might have been experienced travelers or not, we might have several college degrees or none, we might have had rewarding careers in our younger days or not; still, our world has more for us to *do* than we have imagined. Until now, we hadn't the time.

There's one catch to taking advantage of the time and opportunities available now: We must get off the old duff and do it ourselves. No mother or teacher is going to spoon-feed us. This is self-help to the *n*th degree.

Every four years, the Junior League of Pueblo, Colorado, raises thousands of dollars with its Follies. For almost thirty years without a break I had been on stage in one act or another for the League, hamming it up and loving every minute. In 1984, I was performing with my regular group, the Red Hot Mamas. One unforgettable night of dress rehearsal, the woman ahead of me in the make-up line turned to face me.

"I'm glad for a chance to talk to you. I've been wanting to thank you."

Thank me? I was mystified. Never saw this woman before in my life. "Whatever I've done, you're welcome."

She did not laugh. "Four months ago my husband died. I've had an awful time getting hold of myself. I've been sitting in the house all alone.

"Then I read the article in the paper about the Follies, saying the Junior League wanted townspeople to try out. And I remembered watching you in the last Follies when you were on that stage just weeks after your husband had died. At that time I thought, 'She's a gutsy lady.' So, I came to try out even though I've never done anything like this before.

"I'm in the chorus line in three numbers, having a good time, getting out with new people, learning to smile again. So thank you."

We hugged and I cried. She didn't.

How often does it happen, I wonder, that some small thing we do has a real effect—good or bad—on someone we never see? Singing and dancing did a lot for that woman's morale, her sense of her own worth. Even more important, she was doing something she'd not tried before, really turning a corner in her life, making a real change. Her conversation with her fellow performers (I eavesdropped) included plans for getting together after the Follies experience. She was out among 'em again in a way that did not depend upon her husband. She was dropping the safety net, moving on her own steam.

My friend Jenny has been visiting back in Colorado. She lives in Atlanta now. Jenny has been divorced and has been slightly lost, you might say. During her stay in Beulah, we were fascinated because Jenny has been taking a course in magic at Emory University.

"Have you always been interested in card tricks and stuff?" we asked.

"Oh, heavens, no. I just saw the course mentioned in the paper and decided it would be fun, a way to meet interesting people, and something new for me to think about."

Jenny delighted and mystified us with her card tricks, and regaled us with accounts of the class taught by the chairman of IBM—the International Brotherhood of Magicians. Now we're all trying the tricks on our own families and friends. They think we've gone a little bonkers, but they love us for it.

Jenny also told us of the great time she had as a volunteer clown in the Macy's Parade in Atlanta. In costume and clown make-up, Jenny and a woman who works with her marched all the way down Peachtree Street. Glorious.

Now her old associates in Colorado are taking a second look at their own lives. Maybe the State Fair Parade or the rodeo . . . this is *networking,* and it works.

With our eyes and ears open, we can find new and marvelous things to do, then pass the magic along to other women like us.

It works especially well in my life in the writing field, but we'll discuss those details in a later chapter. For now, let's examine the ways we can all expand our circles of friends and our areas of interest:

1. Community colleges and state universities offer reduced tuition for seniors and special courses for "returning students." Included here are the Elderhostel programs. Any school or library can help you with detailed information. Courses include those subjects you want to study for your own satisfaction (languages, anthropology), as well as practical stuff like computers.

2. Libraries all over the country are getting into the act with "writers in residence" and readings of local poets, etc. Also big in libraries these days are the film series, if you are more passive about knowledge but enjoy something more stimulating then reruns of *Dallas*.

3. Local art museums are running more and more excursions to near-by major galleries and exhibitions as well as sightseeing trips based on a common interest in architecture and art. Go along, by yourself the first time if you have to. There will be congenial fellow passengers looking for much the same lifestyle challenges that intrigue you. Being a docent is okay, of course, but traveling to other museums is more broadening.

4. Some concerts and theater groups offer oldsters the joy of seeing many performances as ushers. This is true at SPAC in Saratoga Springs, with the San Francisco Opera (I understand), and other such quality places. A phone call to any such facility near you cannot cost anything and might open untold new doors in your life.

5. Certainly in every community there are senior centers where you can be entertained, enlightened, or be of service. Any local newspaper can fill in those details.

"But how do you start? I'd be terrified to walk into a college classroom at my age. Weren't you afraid you'd make a fool of yourself?"

I hear a lot of this kind of talk, so I'll tell you about my first days in the classroom at Adirondack Community College.

That fall semester I took Creative Writing, Basic Design, Poetry, and (as I recall) Spanish I. Bear in mind that older students are not as rare now as they were during our school days. I was not the only over-thirty in any of these classes, but the majority of students were just out of high school.

In Creative Writing, I was looked upon as "teacher's pet" because Professor Rikhoff and I had been friends for a year or two before I decided to attend ACC. It took a while for my fellow writing students to accept me as one of the crowd, but it happened gradually. Outside the classroom is where much of Creative Writing pays off, with one-on-one discussions over coffee and such. Those kids didn't want to confide in some imported senior citizen who would go ratting off to the teacher about their problems with assignments. When they realized I had writing problems akin to theirs, the Big Thaw came.

Basic Design did not work out at all. I was the only student with bifocals. This made it impossible to focus on the paper-cutter. The nervous little beard-o who taught the course would instruct us to make all sorts of cut-out combinations of circles, rectangles, squares. Fine. Then we had to put our work up on the board.

All of my rectangles listed to starboard. The squares were innocent of any right angles. The circles resembled hard-cooked eggs. My rubber cement seemed to smear more than that used by more accomplished students. I am a Design Drop-Out.

Spanish class was fun. The professor expected a Coloradoan to have a working knowledge of Spanish, particularly a more-than-middle-age woman from a town with a name like Pueblo. The college bookstore had under-stocked on Spanish texts. I had to wait to buy my book. When Professor Spitzer called on me for a translation, I sat helplessly in the back of the room, blushing because my homework was not done.

"*Porque* (why), *Señora Weaver?*"

He scared me. *"Porque,"* I stammered, trying to recall freshman Spanish from 1941, *"Porque no tengo . . . book-o."* My classmates thought this was hilarious. We were all friends on the spot.

*T*his is a good place to explain to you what kites have done in my life, particularly because anyone honestly wanting a new direction in life can find *something* of interest that might work miracles.

I did say kites. Kites have opened more doors for me, made more new friendships, and started more juices flowing in my life, than anyone would dream possible.

In the first place, kites make friends. Kites become friends. To fly a kite is a challenge and a pleasure to be enjoyed alone or in a crowd. My kite-flying days began in 1974 and will not end until I am totally incapacitated.

Peggy Gandy introduced me to kites when I was fifty years old. She had discovered the Kite Revolution in California—the glorious new twenty-five-foot dragons made of silver Mylar, the German *Schmetterlings,* and the Indian fighter kites. Peggy was a life-enhancer; what she enjoyed, she shared.

Our first kite-fly and picnic was an absolute revelation. Our kites (mine borrowed from a nutty friend) soared, whirled, dipped, and tangled over Ernamarie's pasture like nothing I had seen before.

Four of us were hooked. We became the Beulah Valley Association for Tethered Flight. Three more members were added because they had fine pastures. And my life was changed out there on the Beulah Road, hanging onto a nylon line, thrilled by the antics of a weird-looking nylon half-mattress in the sky.

What if Peggy had said, "I never could get a kite up when I was a kid," and had stuck to her knitting? What if my other friends of the BVATF had scoffed at the idea of women our age flying kites—"That's the silliest thing I ever heard of! Me? Taking time out to have a picnic on a weekday, and try to fly a kite?"

Worst of all, what if we had had an attack of the guilties and had insisted on bringing the kids or the grandchildren along?

What if we had all said, "I'm too old for such nonsense"?

Too old to spend time out in the fresh air with good friends, challenging ourselves to acquire a new skill, find a different pleasure in our surroundings? Too old to study a bit about aerodynamics, nylon lines, and flexible kites that had been invented long after our fumbling attempts at tethered flight with plain old diamond kites made of newspaper and balsa wood? Too old to do something new?

My first writing for publication was about kites. Before that article, the BVATF sponsored kite-flies and festivals occasionally; but, like most kitefliers, we preferred making our own fun with kites as members of the Beulah Valley Association for Tethered Flight.

On cruise ships I have made new friends through kites. Every Christmas, I am delighted with letters from the Binswangers of Philadelphia, the Merritts in Indianapolis, and the Kuhns in Ohio because we flew kites together from the afterdeck of the *Royal Viking Star.*

My mail includes clippings about kites from all over the country. From as far away as New Zealand I have been sent kites as gifts. Little kids stop me on the street to talk about kites. Best of all, I have heard my grandchildren brag in their neighborhoods about my skill with a kite.

Around the world I collected kites, which I exhibit in libraries and schools with great pleasure. In Glens Falls, New York, I am introduced as Fran Weaver, the Kite Lady. On any beach, in any mountain pasture, in any city park, I can be certain of bringing happiness to total strangers with a kite, all because of Peggy and her picnic.

*W*hy tell you this? It can happen in your life, as much or as little as you want whether you choose a craft, a collecting hobby, something more athletic or more artistic, whatever—your life can be the center of an ever-widening circle.

"This is a time of final options," I quoted earlier in this book. Those options can be simple, and simply marvelous.

Fly! you flippant fribbling dragons
Dance toward heaven   seek new heights
Flicker   flutter   float   you eagles
Effervescent in your flight
Soar above capricious breezes
Dart behind a low-slung cloud
Swoop!   you skittish sons of ether
Flitting   gliding   buoyant   proud
Steady as she blows bright Phoenix
Skim above me   lively   free
Ascending as the sunlight beckons
Bait for angels   Wait for me

Moving

Is a Lot Like Making Love

OUR PLACE, OR MINE?

"*I*ve made up my mind. I'm going to stay in our big house one more year. That will make twenty-five years I've lived there. Then I'll move to someplace easier to take care of."

Joanne made this announcement at a dinner party last winter. Nobody had asked her about changing her living arrangements, but the statement seemed necessary for her, right then, in that crowd. We all knew Joanne had been debating the question of moving out of her house for several years since Bill had died and the kids had homes of their own.

Any stranger hearing her incessant conversation about moving would have thought she was deciding to dismantle Mount Vernon or the Hearst Castle. Actually, she lives near the golf course in a nice-enough four-bedroom house with a big yard. A salable property but no showplace.

Around the room at this gathering, we all nodded politely and continued other conversation.

What I wanted to ask was simple. "*Then* what will you do, Joanne? Talk about moving?"

Years ago, I decided that moving is a lot like making love:

1. You hope for satisfaction when it's over.
2. Experience is worth more than advice.
3. The less conversation, the better.

I still feel the same way about this question of changing homes, even as a widow. Particularly as a widow. We do hope for satisfaction from a move, but in different ways than during our mothering, married days. We used to need more bathrooms, larger closets, a family room for the kids, and a separate bedroom for as many as possible. We used to covet big fenced yards for the toddlers to roam in or for the dog to be safe. There used to be a hoop for basketball over the garage as soon as we moved in.

Now, we can be satisfied with less space, but different priorities. An attached garage leading directly to the kitchen would be nice since we carry our own groceries. Fewer steps might be helpful since some of our friends (not us!) are getting along in years. Having less to dust and more freedom from household responsibilities is certainly on the plus side, especially if we have determined to get on with these last twenty years in a style befitting a woman of our intelligence and good sense.

Experience does count for a lot in moving, always. Good or bad, we have learned about houses, apartments, and rental properties. We are able to evaluate our own needs. If experience tells us we need a larger place and a houseful of family "treasures," so be it. If experience tells us housekeeping is not as much fun as it used to be when the family came trooping in saying, "Gee, the house looks nice, Mom" before they messed it all up, then we need to find our fun elsewhere.

Experience has taught us moving can be a headache, but it can be an improvement in our lifestyle and a boost to our egos. Few of us have chosen or furnished a nest of our own on our own. This is stimulating and frightening at the same time. To hang pictures just where we want them, move them without someone yelling about "more holes in the wall," to shift two chairs and one couch a dozen different ways to suit only ourselves, to have pink or orange or puce on the bathroom walls if we like it, to use throw rugs in the bedroom or tape favorite snapshots to the back of the door in the hall—those are options when we have a place of our own, chosen just for us.

If we stumble over the newly moved chair in the dark on the way to the bathroom, we have only ourselves to blame. That's okay. It's a part of being on our own.

Now about number three, the less conversation the better.

Do discuss your choices about moving only with those directly concerned: your children, the rest of your family, and certainly your financial advisor. Then keep your own counsel. As many opinions are available as you might want to find. What we all need in this time of our lives is confirmation, not well-meaning instruction. After too much carrying-on about whose sister was miserable/ecstatically happy in Scottsdale or Sun City, the fun of the decision is gone. The outcome is doomed. Trust yourself about making a move. You know enough to make up your own mind.

My primary reason for moving out of the family home when John died was basic: After the death of my father-in-law, John and I went to Kansas to clear out his parents' house. His mother had died years earlier, but neither of those people had thrown out or disposed of *anything* in the fifty-plus years they lived in that one house on Republican Street in Concordia. Every room of that place was filled with strange collections of things—just things—and memorabilia that broke your heart and your back at the same time.

John had said many times to his father, "Don't you want to get rid of some of this, Joe? You don't need most of these things any more."

Joe's laugh was unforgettable. "That's a lot of trouble for me, Johnny. I'll just leave that for you to do." Like it was a good joke on his only remaining son.

Clearing out drawer after drawer, closet after closet, cupboard after cupboard of long unused stuff, all of the good and bad times of John's life poured over him and there was nobody of his boyhood there to share the joy or the pain.

Size five gypsy costumes for Halloween, the layette of a baby brother who had died, broken Tonka Toy trucks, and medals from long-forgotten track meets. Never had I seen anyone put through such an emotional wringer as my husband went through there. I finally called the thrift shop at the church and the junk hauler. We went home to Colorado, leaving all of those things. That's all they were, things.

I brought home one good keepsake from that lousy trip: the determination that none of my offspring would ever have to go through such an ordeal because of me.

Six months after their dad's death, I issued the summons: "Come and get whatever you want from this house. One week from Monday the Goodwill truck will take the rest." None of us has regretted that decision.

There are some women who seem to think moving from the home provided by their husbands is a sign of disloyalty or lack of appreciation. Some seem to hear a thundering voice from above: "You nagged for years for this house, now you act like you don't want it! Don't you understand how hard I worked so you could have two and a half baths and a built-in dishwasher?"

Times of our lives have changed, ladies. You are on your own now. So am I. What we are really facing is living alone.

ME AND MY SHADOW

*L*iving alone means I can stay up as late as I want to or go to bed without waiting for the ten o'clock news.

Living alone means I can eat all of the Pepperidge Farm cookies without feeling I must hide the empty sack.

Living alone means I can turn on as many lights as I want when I go to the bathroom in the middle of the night.

Living alone means I can listen to talk radio to my heart's content.

Living alone means I feel free to leave the mess of bill-paying out on the dining-room table until I have time to finish the job.

Living alone means I don't have to have a dog.

Living alone means enough smoked oysters in one can.

Living alone means that staying late in town doesn't delay anyone else's dinner.

Living alone isn't a bunch of fun, but living alone is not all bad, for a change. That's what it is for most of us, a change.

Like any change of the cast of characters in our little drama, this brings accommodation to new circumstances. For instance:

Living alone means there's nobody to help carry in the groceries.
Nobody to take out the trash.
Nobody to laugh with over the Cosby show.
Nobody to play gin rummy or share scrapbooks on a rainy night.
Nobody to say, "I love you."
I have learned to buy fewer groceries at one time, to use very small trash bags and make more trips to the bins outside, to ask a friend in for supper on good TV nights, to go to the foreign films or a lecture at an art museum when life alone is honestly a bore, to write lots of letters in the evenings, and to make my writing take up so much of my time and attention that I have little time to be bothered about being alone.

Then I call someone to say, "I love you," and to hear that person say it to me.

During a writers' seminar on aging and women, the question was asked, "Why do so many women choose to live alone after sixty?"

Statistics were quoted: Of women over sixty, more than half of us are widows and eighty per cent of us live alone. Very few older men live alone, maybe twelve per cent. Aside from the expected "I don't want to be a burden to anybody," the answers boiled down to one fact: Widows in their sixties are generally truly single for the first time in their lives.

One sweet-faced little lady in the seminar spoke up: "Listen. Until six years ago, I never had the bathroom or the refrigerator all to myself. I might save money by bunking in with somebody else, but as long as I can manage for myself I'm not giving up my right to do exactly as I please around my own place."

We all nodded approval. We can make what we want of every day on our own, and that's just fine.

The danger of living alone is boredom. Boredom is ninety-nine per cent self-inflicted. I've told you that before.

So living alone brings the freedom, but also the responsibility, for avoiding stagnation. We are self-propelled at this age. Unless we rev ourselves up regularly by getting out among 'em with a real purpose in mind, we'll find ourselves more alone than we intended.

But getting home to peace and quiet certainly is nice.

The Men in Our Lives—
Where?

Senior Singles' Lament

My friend and I would like to dance a bit
To snuggle close in some man's gentle arms
We'd love to hear some 1940s hits
We'll captivate our partners with our charms
We're willing to provide the transportation
We'll surely be the ones to buy the drinks
Our dancing will create a huge sensation
For the guy who finds it's later than he thinks
Our jitterbug will drive the fellows mad
We'll whirl across the floor with style and grace
The dance hall owners surely will be glad
When we come in to liven up the place
Six foot or more will suit us fine for height
Come one, come all, the line forms on the right.

JUST ASK ME TO DANCE. PLEASE!

"*I*t's not the empty nest that's driving me around the bend. It's the empty bed. I'm only sixty years old. I'm still a young woman as far as—"

Believe it or not, I hear this and similar complaints often when I'm talking to women my age, particularly widows. One woman even said, "I thought I'd be glad to be rid of the sex part of my life, but I really miss it."

One of my favorite descriptions of my own age has been, "I'm so old I've never even *seen* a StayFree Maxi Pad." That's always good for a laugh, but invariably some older woman brings up one of the indisputable facts we have to live with: Most men in their fifties or older prefer younger women.

Why? We have our own teeth; our shapes are no worse than those of fifty-plus men; we appreciate warmth and affection more than we ever did when we were harried housewives chasing muddy children or trying to keep peace in the neighborhood. We certainly don't have to fret about waking the kids or having more of them any more. So why do men always seem to prefer women in their thirties or forties or twenties, even?

And why do I find my teeth on edge and the hackles rising on the back of my neck when I'm walking down the street with a man my own age who not only pauses to openly admire some bra-less girl in her tight jeans and ridiculous spike heels but has the temerity to remark about such beauty? That's the way men are.

As with many other phases of widowhood in this book, I have my own theory. What do you think of this? Ask a little boy who's the prettiest woman he knows. He'll say "Mommy" most of the time. Ask a young man the same question. He'll name the love of his life, his young bride. These prettiest women are in their twenties. They both take care of him, pamper him, ask him what he wants for breakfast, and kiss him when he skins his knee.

When his prettiest mother gets older, he is a teen-ager arguing with her about staying out late or having a couple of beers. When his prettiest wife gets older, he sees her as a nagging wife who argues with him about their teen-agers and the car and has a fit when he has a couple of beers. Or she suggests that he fix his own breakfast.

When this man we're talking about was a youngster, there was probably some shrewish old crow on his block who wore pink print zipper-front housedresses and bedroom slippers, had her hair on curlers or in a net, and yelled at him for riding his bike on her sidewalk or playing cops and robbers in her shrubbery. That is his immutable idea of an older woman, and men's impressions are not easily changed. That's why men prefer young women. They always have. Simple, but I have yet to find anyone who can prove me wrong in this theory or even argue about it.

The few men who appreciate older women are more flexible in

their opinions or feel more secure with their own age. I happen to think they're a lot smarter. Another prejudiced personal opinion.

So, what's a ladylike, well-brought-up woman in her sixties or seventies to do with this situation? We are not about to hang around singles bars or place personal ads in the local newspaper. Happily, there are more and more places to go dancing to music of the '40s, more centers where oldsters gather one at a time. Risk-takers can find some solutions in those situations. Others sit at home and moan, or refuse to admit the true nature of their frustration. "I wouldn't want a man around again except for companionship," some old ladies will blush to tell you.

One other indisputable fact is operable in this discussion: There aren't as many old men as there are old women, no matter how they feel about the aging ladies. No matter how many diets we suffer through or how many stress fractures we endure in aerobics dance classes in order to fit into girlish dresses and look cute in shorts, no matter how we might study up on the Denver Broncos or the New York Mets just to carry on a conversation with a man, finding an available man to talk to is next to impossible sometimes. Finding one who finds us physically desirable is a downright miracle.

This subject came up during a counseling session I had with a young psychologist during a stress-management clinic. In the first place, he seemed astonished when I was pretty blunt about such matters. He probably assumed that at my age I'd forgotten about all that. I explained that a man doesn't have to sign a pre-marital agreement just to hug me, or worry about paying my supplemental Medicare insurance because we go together to a fine restaurant where I cannot go alone.

"Any man's future is a lot safer in a free-wheeling, slightly more than casual relationship with a woman my age than getting involved with a sweet young thing who will saddle him with three half-grown kids and a mother-in-law his own age," I told him.

That poor red-faced young man looked as if he might cry. When I finally shut up, he said, "Don't you have any prospects?"

I laughed. "No, sonny, I don't. That's one reason I keep myself so busy, so satisfied with the rest of my new life, so surprised about what I can accomplish on my own, that I have no time to lie around feeling unloved in that sense of the word."

The universality of the feelings of older women hit me hardest in a conversation with a seventy-year-old man who lives with his wife in a Leisure World back east. I was working on a proposed novel about people in retirement communities at the time, and he agreed to be interviewed.

"You'll have to include the sex life," was his first remark, much to my surprise. "Not only the old men. Of course, we're still interested. That's a big part of our lives now. But I feel sorry for the women because so many of them are alone. You ought to see them. The minute some old guy's wife dies, the casserole brigade begins. All they want is to feel wanted, loved, warm again. Seems like they all want one more orgasm," he said thoughtfully.

Writers of books about aging usually insist upon the continuation of sexual drive and satisfactions as long as we are in good health, but few have any concrete suggestions for fulfilling these desires. My new mentor, B. F. Skinner, approaches the subject warily:

"It is too bad that affectionate relations between people of different ages are viewed uneasily. It is hard to see what is wrong with love between people of different ages, provided it is mutual." Then he changes the subject. That takes us right back to the first of this chapter—old men and young girls, or vice versa, though Skinner does not say so.

In absolutely practical approaches to the dilemma of enduring sexual desire in women past the age when they can logically expect another marriage or even a lover, I am reminded of the most successful gynecologist in Kansas City, many years ago. Some of his clientele were patients who had depended on him for treatment and advice for years. This wonderfully understanding physician had special "examining rooms" in his office equipped with vibrators where older women came for twenty-minute appointments for self-administered therapy.

In a doctor's office, that sort of thing was okay. At home, it was unthinkable. His patients adored him for his thoughtfulness.

Since beginning the final draft of this chapter, I have talked with three or four friends of my own age. The responses when I mentioned this chapter are worth recording here.

"Well, it's nice to spend the afternoon in bed when you both feel like it. Much less pressured than when we were younger. More concern for each other."

"Just tell your readers it's a lot better after sixty than it ever was before."

And, "What's your problem writing about sex? You forgot?"

WILT THOU TAKE THIS . . . ?

*O*kay. Let's talk about remarriage. It surely works for a lot of people. I considered it once, myself, and my attitude now is slightly negative. However, like the Methodist ministers of my youth, I am "reminded of the words of that fine old song, 'I'll never say never again again.'" Marriage is a fine institution for folks who feel the need.

Feel the need I did, over ten years ago when I met a nice little man on a cruise of the Panama Canal. He was a widower, soft-spoken, amiable, loved my jokes. Our breakfasts together on board ship were a delight. We promised to see each other again. Just friends.

After I had visited him once at his house and he had stopped over in Colorado to spend a few days with me, we were more than friends. The contrast of our relationship with my thirty-four-year marriage was startling and refreshing. We did not argue about anything, particularly my kids or my bank account. There were none of the old marriage conflicts which I had despaired of so often with John. I thought marriage to this man would be one idyllic journey of serenity for both of us. He figured out what I had on my mind, and refused to consider marrying me. Thank God for that.

During the next year we did some traveling together, my writing started to flourish, and the difference in our ages really began to take its toll. He was older. As he became happier with the sedentary life of "comfy evenings at home" when I had driven two hundred miles to spend a weekend, I realized I was right back at it, watching TV while the man in my life snored on the couch.

An extended trip together put the end to the relationship. Any man who complains about my kite-collecting and tries to tell me how to spend what's mine has lost the old ball game. His constant bragging about the fact that he had never allowed anyone, even his wife, to drive his precious car was the final turnoff. Regrettably, by that time he had decided marriage was a good idea.

From that experience I can say, without reservation, breaking up a relationship is no better or easier at fifty-eight than it was in junior high school. The old hurts, the vulnerability, are terrible. Lesson learned: Tread carefully when a new more-than friendship looms on the horizon, or just peeks at you across the dinner table some Saturday night.

On another cruise, I met the unforgettable widower who made a lasting negative impression. He was preparing a questionnaire for all of the women desperately wanting to marry him. He considered himself such a great catch, he was being very careful to avoid gold-diggers or women who just wanted the prestige of a husband as handsome, wealthy, and altogether wonderful as he knew he was. He would place a blind ad in selected newspapers (*The Wall Street Journal?*) and have his attorneys screen the applicants for the position of Mrs. Marvelous.

He confided the first two questions:

1. How much money do you have?
2. Do you get seasick?

Imagine that! I have never heard what sort of response his ad elicited, but I hope he got a real dog. With bad breath. There are possible areas of conflict that must be ironed out the second time around, no doubt about that. Oldsters getting married will not have fifteen or twenty years to work out the kinks in a household. They'd better know each other pretty well before they start shaking orange blossoms at each other.

Here are questions bound to come up in a second marriage that need to be faced squarely by both parties. They are based on my own observations and by reflections on those days when the best thing I could say about my husband was, "He married well."

1. What do you feed your dog?
2. Where does your dog sleep?
3. How often do you expect your children to visit?
4. Do you keep family pictures in the living room?
5. How do you feel about small overdrafts?
6. Are you picky about leftovers? Salads? Cheese?
7. What is your idea of a great vacation?
8. Is your mother still living? Near here?
9. Do your children expect you to baby-sit?
10. Can you repair leaky toilets or dripping faucets?
11. Will you dance? Play bridge? Take a walk?

12. Did your first wife bake bread? Make waffles?
13. Do you know how to load the dishwasher? Fold sheets?

That's a start. All of you can finish the list. As for me, at this moment I think I'll prepare a questionnaire for aspiring gigolos. Only a couple of questions would take care of that.

Travel.

When? Where? How?

HEARTS YOUNG, HAIR GRAY

Two little old ladies were pleased to be seated together on a plane bound for Florida. "Ah, I'm happy to see you going to Miami. Last year we didn't see you in Miami."

"Last year we didn't go to Miami."

"So where did you go?"

"To Majorca."

"Oh. So where's Majorca"?

"I don't know. We flew."

Stories of my travels around the world would fill a book more than twice the size of this one. I am an enthusiast, a nut about going places. I always have been.

My husband was not fond of travel just to get away. He loved to work. We stayed closer to home than most of our friends. Together we never went to Europe or even to Mexico. My life in the past fifteen years has been spent playing catch-up with all of the tripping I had not done earlier.

That's all right. John would not have wanted to go "chasing from pillar to post." I can imagine his voice saying just those words when I am buying kites in Bangkok or basking on a Greek beach.

Travel was necessary as a drastic break in the familiar routines of home in order to establish a life of my own after John's death in 1980. During that first year of adjustment I settled for short excursions to visit old friends. Then I took off, starting with a cruise through the Panama Canal.

Years later, I was on a bus bumping over a rough road under construction outside of Beijing watching Chinese road-building crews working with shovels and buckets. My friend Mary and I had dabbled in international shopping in Hong Kong, had toured a Children's Palace in Shanghai, had stood in awe above the excavated terra cotta soldiers guarding the emperor Quin's tomb in Xian, had walked through the Forbidden City and the Summer Palace in Beijing. We had eaten Chinese food we could never describe to the folks back home, including the webbed feet of ducks served to us at a state dinner in the Great Hall of the People. We had flown over mainland China in an old Russian prop jet. We had walked on the Great Wall and posed for pictures beside lions guarding the Ming Tombs.

We were pleasantly tired returning to our cruise ship when our charmer of a Chinese guide announced, "This is a long ride (she said "rong lide") so I entertain you. I sing now." She beamed at us, held the microphone carefully in one hand, waved the other hand gracefully, and began in the flute-like singing voice of the Oriental:

"In a cavern / In a canyon / Excavating for a mine / Lived a miner / Forty-Niner / And his daughter . . ."

She sang at least four verses of "Clementine" with a smile, a tilt of her head, which entranced even the gripers on the bus.

Then she sang familiar songs from *Sound of Music,* with the Chinese accent which reverses *l*s and *r*s in such a wonderful way. When she started on that old American favorite (in her opinion) "Led Liver Varrey," the applause was wild. We sang along. What a privilege and what a joy, I thought. Then she sang Chinese songs and we clapped even more.

Thousands of miles from home, bouncing along on a bus, here I was watching the building of a real rapport with these people from whom we had been isolated for so many centuries. In some strange way I'll never look at my own world through the same eyes again.

Any travel experience can be an eye-opener. You should have seen me with my friend Professor Rikhoff on the beach in Rhodes. A couple of Gibson Girls in Gay Nineties bathing costumes would not have been any more conspicuous. The sky was clear, the water an unbelievable sea green shading into deepest blue. Visible on the horizon was the mountainous coast of Turkey. In close-order rows along the beach were thousands of umbrellas and lounge chairs. And there we stood, wearing our standard American one-piece swim suits—two middle-aged women on a topless beach.

My friend the professor and I were on Rhodes, a stunning semitropical Greek island that is the Mediterranean mecca for northern Europeans, mostly sun-worshippers. All day long they lie there grilling themselves to a golden turn, clad in nothing more than a G string. We were overdressed, to say the least. We might just as well have been wearing one-piece black woolen Jantzens with red diving girls on the skirts.

Maybe we would have looked a little better without the shoes. Hot sands and rocky beaches of other islands prompted us to sport Chinese slippers, the ones that look like "Mary Janes." The professor had on her Gertrude Ederle swim cap, which didn't do a lot for the image, either.

One glance up and down the beach made it chillingly clear. We had the only covered bosoms on the whole beach, a beach that stretched for at least two miles. In forty years of practice, my gynecologist did not examine as many bare breasts as we saw on that beach in one hour. Those sauna-weary Scandinavians are the least self-conscious people I have ever seen.

My first feeling was outrage. Have they no shame? Then I tried to be cosmopolitan—cultural folkways are of interest to world travelers, I told myself. Then I remembered a class in comparative anatomy, but it was nothing like those girls parading on the sand. When I spotted women my age and older who had also shed their modesty, I gave up. Too bad they didn't.

There are many expressions about being in the minority. "Bastard at a family reunion," and such. We felt that much out of place among those nearly naked beauties, but we persevered, determined to get a tan.

That out-of-place feeling paled soon afterward when we found ourselves a part of the backpack set—and there is nothing like a night in a pension in Turkey to reinforce appreciation of the Good Life.

My friend the professor and I learned that lesson the hard way trying to be Mother Good Sport to a couple of backpackers.

"Now this is going to be fun. We can put up with anything for one night; and it's cute of these kids to invite us to team up with them, a real adventure." We kept telling each other such nonsense as our new friends led us to the rooms they had found in Marmaris, a minuscule seaport on the Aegean coast of Turkey. The bus to Ephesus was full, so we were spending the night. Our first look at the chosen pension—

double rooms with shower for three dollars—should have been enough; but the girl from Chicago had said, "There are a lot of steps," in a manner suggesting we oldsters might need assistance. That was a challenge not to be ignored.

The landlady was a delight and beside herself with the prospect of four American guests. She ran ahead up more steps—into No. 2, motioning the professor and me to follow. No. 2 was a dingy green room with four cots, no rugs, three old bedspreads tacked up for curtains, a bare bulb hanging from exposed wiring in the middle of the ceiling, and a picture of Ataturk in one corner.

The professor stared at the four cots, then at the Danish boy who had become our fellow traveler.

"Oh, no, Danny! Not four to a room!"

"Paula and I will be next door. Don't worry."

To find the shower, we were led through No. 1, back outside, down the steps, thence into a concrete cave equipped with a shower head suspended from the ceiling not two inches from another bare light bulb on an extension cord. Electrocution in a Turkish shower crossed my mind. The toilet was up on our floor past No. 3, the last room. It was that gem of modern Turkish plumbing, an indoor porcelain slit trench with a bucket.

It felt like camping, but we were tired enough to sleep.

I wakened, certain it was time to get up, and tiptoed to the bathroom to look at my watch. Ten minutes after twelve. I stole a sheet from No. 1 for a cover and went back to bed. In another two weeks it was four-thirty, and the professor said she'd dreamed she was digging a bed for herself in some dirt.

As if cots made of cardboard and sand and chill breezes were not enough, there were the noises. One demented rooster crowed all night.

Donkeys brayed. Dogs fought. There were bells and whistles and mo-torbikes. A constant drip filled the bucket by the toilet.

The next night we checked into the most expensive hotel in Ku-sadasi, Turkey, a medieval fortress of great beauty and charm and mod-ern plumbing built to be a stop for caravans in the fifteenth century. No camel driver was ever happier to hit that place than we were.

Get Set . . . Go!

*T*ravel is not simply seeing new places. We've always known that. Now travel becomes even more important to us in widening our horizons at the time in our lives when time is what we have the most of.

There's no need for a woman in her sixties to go all the way to China to expand her horizons. Unless you live in the middle of Death Valley, there is someplace interesting—even new—for you to explore within a day's drive of your home—perhaps half a day.

Try this, for example: Spread a road map of your area on the table. Draw a circle with a three-hundred-mile radius around your home with a jar lid or a small dish. Within that circle you'll find all sorts of out-of-the-way places to go and things to do.

Second step in the process is to call a couple of friends and arrange a day trip or a two-day trip just for fun. Choose a new place or return to old haunts, but *go*. That's a start toward weekends, group tours, travel clubs, cruises, specialized excursions, off-season bargains—even getting into the travel business yourself.

Before we go any further, let's get one thing straight: Traveling with other women is not the same as traveling with a man. We all know that, too. From luggage-handling to dancing on cruise ships, from dining in fine restaurants to understanding the rate of exchange, there's nothing like having a man at your side. We have to accept that fact and adjust our expectations. Then we can have a good time.

Women of our age are used to the protection of having a man around. We are not the most liberated or self-sufficient generation. We were not raised that way. We also appreciate the fact that men can be impatient shoppers, picky about the way their eggs are cooked, and absolutely impossible when it comes to asking directions after making a wrong turn.

It is not unusual these days for unmarried couples to travel together. That can work very well to the advantage of both parties, as the saying goes. This is a new freedom for people our age, and more power to you if you can make it work for you.

Here's an example of what can happen, however.

I was in New York with a bachelor friend whom I had known for years. We were going up in the elevator in a fine hotel. Two men were in the elevator with us.

"Oh, *nuts!*" said I. "I left my purse on the floor beside my chair in the restaurant."

My companion smiled and pushed the button to stop the elevator at the next floor. "No trouble," said he. "We'll go right over and get it. It's okay. Don't worry." He patted my shoulder. The two men gave me a knowing stare.

Outside the elevator I turned to my old friend. "Now look here! If we're going to travel around looking like we're married, you'll have to shape up your act."

He seemed confused. "In that elevator, you were supposed to yell at me and say things like, 'Can't you hang on to anything?' or 'This is the third time this week you've lost that blasted purse!'"

He understood. But I didn't lose my purse again.

A man who is not your husband might not enjoy hanging around while you choose gifts for eight grandchildren. That depends on how charming *you* are, I suppose, and how many grandchildren he has to shop for. Those are the choices we face in our new world.

I see nothing wrong in being a tourist or looking like one. Tourist attractions have that name because there is something there worth seeing or doing. Now that we do not have children in school or any other valid reason to take vacations only at the height of anyone's season, we can save money and stress by traveling after the crowd leaves or before it gets there.

I act like an absolute tourist most of the time, except when it comes to the camera. Then I try to be nicer—not like those boorish fiends who take hours and hold up traffic trying to get a perfect shot of something already immortalized on ten thousand postcards. I take a lot of pictures in very little time out of the windows of buses and standing on street corners, hoping for decent snapshots from at least one third of the exposures. No sense in overloading my expectations.

Lately my photographic adventures have been fascinating. I double-exposed one half of a film when I was in Oxford. This made for astonishing superimposition of statues on church steeples—a hit at any supper party.

My other adventure with the camera was pure altruism. At the entrance to Mesa Verde National Park, I spied a family of young Japanese. The father was taking a picture of the mother and two adorable round-faced children. I pulled my car to the shoulder of the road in a hurry and rushed up to the young man, offering in my best sign language to snap a picture of the family together. I can still hear myself:

"You stand with children? I take picture for you?"

I went into my imitation of a charades game, waving my hands in his face, pretending to hold, aim, and operate the Nikon in his hand. He smiled gratefully and ran to stand beside his wife and kids. When I handed back the camera, he thanked me politely. He was a pediatrician from Seattle, or some such place.

When I got back in the car my granddaughters said, "That was really nice of you to be so helpful to our foreign visitors, Oma."

I probably blushed. "They were Americans, Sarah, just like you and me. I hope I didn't insult them with my silly antics. I should have spoken English to them to find out who they were."

Back to the subject of off-season travel: Airline rates are always lower; so are hotel rates. This is not to suggest spending time in Florida or Palm Springs in the middle of July, but early autumn is good weather almost anywhere. So is late spring.

Sensible planning is part of the game, whether we go alone or with a group. My friend Professor Rikhoff and I planned almost a year for our trip to Greece, Italy, and France in 1984. She planned much more than I did. Consequently she got much more from the two-month experience because she had crystallized her expectations. I learned a lot from that.

Travel magazines and the travel sections of the big newspapers are full of ads and information, specific and general, about any place we can think of and some we've never heard of. There are also tourist bureaus in New York and California representing almost any country in the world, particularly those with their own airlines. They are more than eager to send information to prospective tourists; so is the travel and tourism bureau of every state in the union. The addresses of these bureaus can be found through libraries or your travel agent.

Then there are the travel guides, *Europe on Twenty Dollars a Day,* and all that. A travel guide is not unlike a book about raising your baby. Nobody should have more than one such book. The conflicting advice in two or more might ruin your trip. The professor and I must have had fifty pounds of travel guides that we dragged to Greece. Every time we decided to move from one island to another we consulted local pamphlets plus Frommer, Fodor, American Express, and the Harvard guide for the backpack set.

We found the Class B hotels to be clean, adequate, and fairly well located, but universally without luggage handlers. The books had not told us that. I should have had a garage sale before we left Athens to go to the islands because I carried at least three times too much stuff.

We also stumbled onto some dandy beach hotels not mentioned in any book and some great food at next-to-nothing prices just by wandering in on our own. Our expert advice about travel guides is to decide on one you trust and throw the others away.

One of our more memorable restaurant finds was a tavern sitting alone on a hill on the far side of Mykonos, our first Greek island. The manager/chef/owner/waiter gleefully escorted us to his kitchen. We were to point out the food we wanted. Wonderful. We chose a huge fish to be grilled.

The professor sign-languaged a request for a napkin by pointing to her lap. Our host brought an oversize apron, tied it around her, and presented us with a huge fish to deal with in any way we could. We laughed and made real sport of dissecting the fish. The Greeks dining there laughed too, and the food was great.

An American girl at a table in the corner admired our apparent ease of communication and shouted in pure anguish, "Now can one of you women explain to this man that we want three fried eggplant?" We could not.

We rented a car on Crete, where we saw amazing sights like the Lassithi Plain, where there had once been ten thousand windmills (and where the door on our rented Fiat refused to close). On a public beach on Crete we were fascinated by an English woman who stomped onto the sand fully clothed—hat, skirt and blouse, stockings, and heavy shoes. From a shopping bag she pulled a pup tent of pink toweling. She stuck her head, hat and all, through a drawstring hole in the pink tent, covering herself from head to toe. Then she went into some kind of a Houdini-like gyration that made the pink tent look like a gunny sack filled with live chickens. Dropping the portable pink cabaña with one pull of the drawstring, she calmly walked off into the water wearing her swim suit, leaving us sitting there on the sand, speechless.

In Greece, Italy, and France we drove rented cars, which afforded us a great deal of freedom to explore wonderful art museums and archeological wonders without getting involved in organized tours that waste so much time. Being in a car was a challenge because roads were not marked at all well in Greece and my map-reading in Italy and France left a lot to be desired. It was fun, however, and served our purpose for this kind of a trip. We saved money by being able to shop around for hotel rooms and to carry food for lunch along the road.

A word of caution about long hours and distances in a car with just two of you: That's a lot of togetherness. Beware of frazzled nerves and long silences. Those are facts of life to be reckoned with. Travel by car is generally easier if there are more than two of you without crowding the car or the trunk space.

A good system of rotation came out of a driving trip with two of my sisters. Each person drives a hundred miles in a stretch. No more. Then, by the side of the road, everyone gets out and stretches, does a few knee bends, and generally unwinds. The driver moves to the back seat; whoever has been riding front seat takes the wheel; the back-seat person moves to the front.

Duties are explicit. The driver does nothing but drive—no air conditioning or fiddling with the radio. That's the job of the front-seat passenger, who is also the navigator. The back-seat person is the resting driver, also in charge of snacks. Carry along crossword puzzles or "Trivial Pursuit" cards for dull stretches of road. Miles fly by.

This is only the beginning, girls. Whether you're going to take a powder to Boston for chowder or a kayak to Quincy or Nyack, you'll learn more about this as you travel on your own.

ABOVE AND BEYOND THE
FRUITED PLAIN

*K*atherine Lee Bates must have enjoyed her stint "in residence" at Colorado College in Colorado Springs in 1895. We might even assume the clean Colorado air, blue skies, and the Rockies inspired this woman from Falmouth, Massachusetts, beyond her fondest hopes. Safe assumption since she descended from her journey to the top of Pikes Peak and immediately wrote her best-known poem, "America the Beautiful."

Some of us try to claim that song as our own here in Colorado. This attitude seldom wins friends, but I can tell people who ask about Pueblo, Colorado, that I live on the Fruited Plain just below the Purple Mountain's Majesty.

My intention in this chapter is to write about the many places I have seen and enjoyed. Following my own advice about "widening horizons" has led me far, far from the Fruited Plain in the past four or five years. Most of all, I want to share some of the better places I have picked for older travelers, places that seem to me to be better suited for us.

Considerations involved: Simple. We have more time to spend since we're not limited by school vacations or getting back to the office. We understand that getting there can be half the pleasure if we take our time. Most of us recognize the facts of today's world—the easier a place is to get to, the more crowded it will be.

Let's consider first our reason for travel. My favorite travel writer, Pico Iyer, says it best: "What we seek when we journey is a break not so much from our homes as from our habits. The real voyage of discovery consists not in seeing new landscapes but in seeing with new eyes." (Quoting Proust here.) "Travel for us is a sedative as much as a stimulant." He said all this in *Condé Nast Traveler* in September 1994, referring to his own sojourns at a monastery in Northern California.

Not fully aware of the benefits of monastic life, I have found other places that seem just right for me. Certainly any list I compile depends entirely on personal experience. No way can I consider myself a travel expert. The experts produce marvelous detailed guides. All you'll get from me might give you an idea of the sort of place to look for next time you venture forth in search of a "break from our habits."

First and foremost: The Chautauqua Institution on Lake Chautauqua, New York. This venerable, wondrous colony defies description to strangers, but "A Summertime Center for the Arts, Religion and Recreation" begins to tell the story. One of the leaflets in my collection states (on a page featuring a picture of Victorian cottages on a tree-lined brick walk): ". . . the Chautauqua Institution offers an enriching blend of culture and recreation, intellectual vitality and energetic fun." Also: ". . . attracting visitors for more than a century . . ." And: "An ideal vacation destination for the whole family."

Best of all, and this certainly reflects my own opinion of Chautauqua, "You can enjoy what you please as the mood strikes you." Lectures by well-known thinkers, concerts, theater and dance, art, sculpture, even book-binding plus golf, tennis, and water sports surround us in an atmosphere of serenity and an appreciation of the good things in life. Pico Iyer's seeing with new eyes happens at Chautauqua to people of all ages. No motor traffic inside the grounds to "noise up" the calm atmosphere, but the number of strollers for infants and walkers for oldsters is about even, and children ride the trolleys or their bikes around the grounds without fear or hesitation.

Just to emphasize the continuity of the Chautauqua Spirit: At least one third of the audience of six thousand in the amphitheater stood when the master of ceremonies asked, "How many people here have been to Chautauqua every year of your lives?" Little kids and old men stood with pride, and we newcomers (four times for me) wept with pride in being in such a place.

Where? How to get there? Chautauqua lies south of Buffalo on NY Route 394 between Mayfield and Jamestown, east of Lake Erie. The drive is simple from the Buffalo airport and most pleasant coming from Eastern New York through and past the Finger Lakes, Erie Canal, Cooperstown, and so on. Why miss the wonders of New York State when you're already in the area?

For information about program, accommodations, and more, write Chautauqua Institution, Chautauqua, NY 14722 or phone 716/357-6200. Tell 'em Fran Weaver sent you! One pamphlet they will send is "Visitor Guidelines and Responsibilities" including "Please do not disrupt Chautauqua's tranquility."

One other Chautauqua institution I know about and have enjoyed: Lakeside in Ohio. A great place for shuffleboard.

It took me almost sixty years to discover the beauty of New York State. The Adirondacks offer quiet vacation spots on crystal lakes for anyone willing to drive a little to see a lot. My own favorites: Blue Mountain Lake with its outstanding museum, villages of Schroon Lake, Long Lake, Indian Lake, or the busier Lake George at the quiet (north) end. Fort Ticonderoga and Lake Champlain lead us into the joys of Vermont's hills, lakes, and those wonderful meadows with black-and-white cows. One thing a Westerner notices about Vermont: the cows match. I like that.

All of this North Country abounds in scenic landscapes as well as historical sites and fine craft fairs and so on. Autumn certainly attracts the most visitors, so you might find the spring or summer better. Do not ignore Western Massachusetts, like Stockbridge, where the Norman Rockwell Museum and the concerts at nearby Tanglewood thrill even the most jaded of travelers. If you love to drive, do not miss the Taconic Parkway just east of Albany south to Connecticut.

One more fascination of my own in this area is the New York Canal System. We can rent canal boats and pilot ourselves through the locks of the Champlain, Erie, Oswego, and Cayuga-Seneca Canals on a leisurely (ten mph) trip through history. The boats I've seen carry six comfortably. You and your friends could have a different vacation for not much money and have a lot to tell the folks back home. Write to NYS Canal Corporation c/o NYS Thruway Authority, P.O. Box 189, Albany, NY 12201-0189 (518/436-3175).

Bed-and-breakfast and country inn directories come in handy in planning Northeast travel.

Equal opportunities abound around the country, of course. I had a great time with friends on Lopez Island in the San Juans out of Seattle. Again, quiet surroundings with plenty to do as the spirit might move. This especially delighted me because of the ferry ride. In some former life I must have been a whale or something.

Lopez Island's rocky coast and twisted trees made an indelible impression, as did long walks through woods and along the beaches. No rush, no hurry. And the food! Fresh mussels and other seafood served in small friendly places where the waiters were not snobbish and the prices were understandable made my stay outstanding. I hope those folks invite me back.

Other islands? Why not? An Elderhostel on Jekyll Island in Georgia introduced me to another scenic part of our world that offers a slowed-down lifestyle with lots of history. The importance of Georgia in colonial America had escaped my attention until I saw Christ Church on St. Simons Island reminding me that Georgians had been there long before Scarlet O'Hara. The first preacher in that simple, elegant white frame church was John Wesley. The British placed those settlements there to discourage the Spanish moving north of Florida. I didn't know that.

The Georgia Conservancy has a fine book about the Georgia Coast (with a preface by Eugenia Price, herself a great source of information and history of the region in her books) that includes driving tours and such. "Each traveler of the Georgia coast has the opportunity to discover an area rich in history, unusual in its ecosystems, and prized for its relative absence of the effects of man." Seems to me wandering among moss-draped live oaks, broad tidewater rivers, and miles of white sandy beaches ought to provide both the stimulant and sedative effects desired by Pico Iyer and the rest of us seekers of the good life.

The Caribbean Islands—seven thousand of them—offer all sorts of stimulation or sedation, depending upon the accessibility and the number of cruise ships in their harbors. The outer, less-famous islands with their warm breezes and slowed-down way of life appeal to me more than St. Thomas or the busier ports. On islands like St. Barts or Montserrat, the vacationer generally rents a villa for a week or two. Daily invasions of tourists do not bother these smaller islands.

On Aruba, for instance, grand hotels line the beaches, and snorkelers abound. In Montserrat (British) in the Lesser Antilles, no fine hotel of international fame can be found, no Gucci or Armani shops or special duty-free offers of Waterford Crystal confront the visitor. Instead, we rent a three-bedroom, two-bath open-air house with a maid to make the beds, a pool to lounge in beside the front porch, a sweeping lawn down to the Caribbean where one or two sailboats make a busy day. The last bunch of tourists arriving all at once on Montserrat must have been the guys off the *Nina, Pinta,* and *Santa Maria* when Columbus named the island in 1493.

You might prefer Aruba. But for genuine relaxation, no casinos, no stoplights, no loud music or motorscooters buzzing through the night, I'll take Montserrat or other quieter places. Besides, these quieter places cost less than those high-rise resorts. For information about islands like this, try Pace Communications, 485 Fifth Avenue, New York, NY 10017 (212/818-0100).

Villa-renting life can be enjoyed in Europe, as many of my friends point out. Tuscany or Provence might better be appreciated from a semi-permanent housing rather than touring from one hotel to another. Smithsonian or Elderhostel trips to those rather wonderful places would, it seems to me, be the way to explore the possibilities. Then we can make up our own minds about how best to learn the most and see the best. Some of us might like shopping in the local markets and getting acquainted with the townfolks. Others might rather experience the life they have read about in travel magazines or glimpsed on "Lifestyles of the Rich and Famous."

Consult *National Geographic Traveler* and other good travel magazines for details. I also have contacted an outfit called At Home Abroad, 405 East 56th Street, Suite 6-H, New York, NY 10022-2466, and found them to be most helpful.

The most wonderful addition to my own life came with my lecturing on board Crystal Cruises, which I mentioned in an earlier chapter. Cruise life with no baggage-lugging, no discussion over who had the most expensive lunch, and no daily chores (when our greatest decision might be choosing between dance lessons and bridge lectures) fills the bill for me. Both sedating and stimulating as the days progress, with interesting port lectures and fine entertainment besides. Although not a steady diet, cruise life appeals more with every voyage.

Closer to home, we should never lose sight of the benefits of day-tripping from our own place. European or Caribbean trips have to be special, but one or two days in familiar territory enjoying our own space can make a difference in our own outlook. Earlier I described my jar-lid theory of day-tripping. Pay attention, wherever you live. Now that the kids are grown and our weekdays are free, just go.

In compiling a list of attractive, manageable vacation spots for our older set, I must include such splendid areas as Door County in Wisconsin, Mackinac Island in Michigan, Yellowstone Park in winter, the Oregon Coast, the Hill Country of Texas, Northwest Arkansas, and the Ozarks.

To the surprise of some of my stick-in-the-mud acquaintances, I must admit one of my favorite places to enjoy whenever I have the chance is the Epcot Center in Florida. Several times during speaking/book tours in that area, I have gone to Epcot by myself to enjoy the Japanese restaurant, the English village, the movie of France, the feel of the Moroccan marketplace, the Japanese garden, and much more. Too often we consider such family-entertainment places too much for our slower walk, our elderly tastes. Not so here. The very neatness and the pleasant people satisfy me.

Enough of this listing. Almost any of us have favorite uncrowded places if we choose the right time of year, remembering that "off-season" can be even more rewarding, and "close to home" serves Pico Iyer's purpose when we think about it.

Now if you will promise not to tell too many people, I can tell you that the Fruited Plain meets most of my requirements. Here in Southern Colorado we have gorgeous scenery without scary hairpin turns or steep winding roads, our mountains and our Sand Dunes rest the eye and soothe the spirit, our sunny days far outnumber the stormy ones, and our snow evaporates almost before it hits the ground. Roads are good, but traffic isn't that bad.

Movie stars and name-droppers love the splendid resorts where after-ski clothes count most in the wardrobe and being recognized means more than making the run on the slopes. My Colorado features such wonders as cresting a long hill to find Westcliff, safe and serene in the Wet Mountain Valley, basking in the glory of the Sangre de Cristos. Once a rainbow followed me as I drove across the San Luis Valley. The river at the Sand Dunes runs two inches deep and two blocks wide in the early summer. The golf course at Cucharas looks good even if I can't hit a straight shot, even at a driving range.

South of us, Northern New Mexico still evokes an almost spiritual sense of serenity, particularly the light, which is much like the sunlight of the Greek Islands. But charm has given way to commerce in many places.

What have I left out of this chapter? The cities, the resorts, the places where a special fare gets you every amenity known to man or beast from a heart-shaped bathtub to champagne breakfast on the waterfront. If the rates are cut, Folks, it's a cut-rate place where serenity doesn't count.

All in all, the opportunities for enriching our own lives at our own pace and under our own conditions fill our horizons. Look back to those quotes from Pico Iyer that started this chapter, then enjoy. It's our world, don't miss it.

Of Slow Boats and Taking Notes

*O*ther forms of travel? In my opinion, a woman alone should try a cruise at least once. Settled on board, your clothes are in the closets and drawers and your transportation, hotel, meals, and entertainment are all pre-arranged and pre-paid. No luggage to lug, no buses to board unless you opt for the shore excursions.

I love cruise life. You meet basically nice people with whom you have something in common. I have friends all over the country whom I have met on cruise ships. It's a camaraderie I've learned to appreciate.

It is not necessary to fly to the Orient or to Europe to go on a cruise. There are fine small cruise ships on Chesapeake Bay, on the St. Lawrence Seaway, to Mexican ports, in the Inside Passage to Alaska, and of course there's the *Delta Queen* on the Mississippi. There are even three-day cruises from Albany, Buffalo, or Syracuse on the New York State Canal System. (We used to say "barge" but have dropped the term after one hundred sixty years.) There are many other such cruises I have yet to try: those ferries around Vancouver, for example.

A woman need not be a millionaire to take a cruise, but one rule of thumb is valuable if money is a problem—isn't it always? Look for the least-expensive room on the most expensive ship going where you want to go. That is probably the most valuable, useful advice you will get from this book, so pay attention. Also: The longer the cruise, the older the crowd. Women our age tend to prefer the music and entertainment planned for the older crowd, but if you're looking for a younger man . . .

Whatever accommodations or age range you are seeking, take your request to an agent who will take time with you. Find out which of the many cruise ships she (or he) has sailed on, where the agent or others from the office have been. Ask about off-season rates and special promotions. The agent will appreciate your having a written list of questions when you call the office so that travel can be tailored to your tastes.

Feel free to ask for brochures for comparison of stateroom size. And do not be afraid to make a reservation, then change your mind. This is a big adventure and a big expenditure—get what you want from an agent you trust.

The most relaxed people I see while traveling are the folks who have simplified their lives while on the move. Even before I was single, I acted as a tour director for the Colonial Dames of Colorado. We went down the Mississippi and up to Alaska, as well as other trips. Since then I have conducted groups through the Panama Canal and in New England fall foliage.

The travelers who have the least fun are the ones who carry the heaviest purses. God knows what those women have in those satchels, but they hang on for dear life and wear themselves out hoisting their purses onto the bus or into hotel rooms. These are usually the same women who drag along big bargain bottles of shampoo, bulky hair dryers, and six extra sweaters, plus shoes to match every outfit. I have shared rooms with traveling friends who could fill a bathroom counter, the dresser top, and the desk of a hotel room with junk before I unzip my bag. All of this must be moved (often every day), and it weighs a ton. Just once, try a short haircut that can be toweled dry when you travel. It will grow out before anyone asks for your picture. Then bring along one good gray sweater that goes with everything. You'll love yourself for it.

As for those purses, I do wonder what's in them. Identification, a credit card or two, passport, travelers' checks, plus a comb, a lipstick, and some Kleenex should suffice. Just don't take more than you can carry, ever. We live in a world where "red cap" is a forgotten word and "bellhop" is an endangered species.

Simply getting away from home, a change of scenery, is sufficient reason to travel; but an additional interest or purpose is a big plus in choosing a trip. Many women are prone to visit wherever their friends want to go, just to be with the group. They often wind up on a beach when they cannot stand sand between their toes or on an antiques tour not knowing Chippendale from Hepplewhite.

For a while I was on a kick of concentrating on the finest of restaurants and major art museums around the country. A friend and I focused on food and art in Italy, then on our Eastern Seaboard, then in the Far West over a period of almost three years. We put the icing on the cake, literally, when we hopped over to Paris for lunch and wound up spending almost three weeks immersed in the food, sculpture, paintings, and architecture of Paris, Brussels and Brugge in Belgium, plus time in Canterbury and Dover on the way to London.

We did no shopping, theater, or ancient ruins. Those I'll save for another time, but the food and art concentration makes good sense for me now, since my early education had been singularly lacking in art appreciation and my interest in food is overwhelming.

On the home side of the Atlantic, Richard and I have studied museums in Williamstown, Massachusetts, as well as Boston (not only the Museum of Fine Arts but the Isabella Gardner Collection and the Fogg and Busch Reisinger at Harvard). Our restaurants were chosen from critics' columns, not guide books.

In Philadelphia, New York, and Baltimore, we did the same thing, including the Brandywine Museum of the Wyeths in Chadds Ford, Pennsylvania, and Winterthur in Delaware. On that trip we included the fabulous public markets in those cities and the Italian street market in Philadelphia. There's a lot more to see in this country than Mount Rushmore and the Statue of Liberty. Our culinary and art tour moved on to New Orleans, L. A., and San Francisco. Basically, we had one basis of comparison for all of those cities, and I feel qualified to have an opinion now.

I did sort of the same thing on a world cruise in 1983 when I shopped only for kites in every port from Hong Kong to Capetown. It's an approach to traveling I heartily recommend. One of these days I'd like to focus on country inns and private art collections, beginning in the Northeast.

*O*ne great way to tour for specific purpose is with a like-minded group from a museum, historical society, university, or association like the Smithsonian. In this way you have the advantage of having details planned for you and you are assured of congenial company.

Too many women have a tendency to shy away from day excursions of this sort. Give it a try. You might wind up finding someone who, like yourself, would rather travel on his or her own. At least, you'll meet people who want to go someplace instead of sitting in front of the TV all day. Look closely at publications of the National Trust for Historic Preservation, the Oceanic Society, the Smithsonian, and others. They might be headed in the direction you're considering.

For any travel, the most important equipment needed after a passport is a notepad. The smallest-size spiral sketch pads serve the purpose very well because they have a heavy backing and are well-bound. Only with on-the-spot note-taking is it possible to sort out one day or one city from another. The notes need not be full-fledged diaries or journal entries. A word or two will suffice. Recall from these notes is pleasant and amazingly accurate.

It's fun to remember asparagus served on a tilted plate in Bournemouth, trout with tomato butter at La Musardiere in the south of France, salmon with lemon on a bed of fresh spinach at Chez Camille in France; the shorthand jotted in among the notes about Cezanne's walk in Aix. There are also underlined reminders about zucchini rellenos in Taos, New Mexico, and a marvelous lunch at the Mocha Cafe in Denver. That could be useful some day—my travel notebook—to pass along information, if nothing else.

The best use of that notepad is compiling the scrapbook of each journey after you get home. This is also a way to get more than double your money's worth from any tripping by reliving every moment as you take collected notes, brochures, local folders, menus, train tickets, some postcards, and your choicest snapshots to mishmash together in some semblance of order in one of those dime-store albums with the big sticky pages. On a long chest in my Beulah house I have lined up a dozen or more of these "safari scrapbooks," hoping someone will rave over them one of these days. Even if nobody ever opens the covers, I've had a fine time collecting, sorting, snickering, and recalling good and bad times on the road and on the high seas.

Not all well-laid plans work out every time. Be prepared. I figured that out about American Express when I landed in London for a short stay and my hotel reservation had been fouled up.

"Now look here, Frances," I told myself after the frustrated desk clerk had explained he had no reservation, no room, and no prospect of one, "you have two days in London. You can spend one day going crazy trying to find a room or you can get out of town to see something else while waiting for your cut-rate travel agent's crossing on the QE2."

The girls at American Express were just like the commercials. "We certainly can help you locate a hotel at the seaside close to Southampton, where you will board the ship."

"Good show, old girl," I said under my breath. "London will still be here when you come again with more time to see the city, anyway."

Instead of a setback, or a dismal time in a huge city, I did enjoy the seaside town of Bournemouth for a couple of easy days. After all, Paddington Bear prefers Bournemouth.

Incidentally, being a lone traveler in time of such small crisis is an advantage. Two or three of us would have stood around for hours saying, "Well, I don't care. What do *you* want to do?"

That English adventure brings us back to cruises, particularly the QE2. She's a famous ship, and many of her passengers rave about her, but I will choose a smaller, one-class vessel every time. In my opinion, you might as well ride across the ocean in a replica of downtown Dallas as pay such an extraordinary amount of money just to be able to tell your bridge group or the Friday night poker set about "The *Queen.*"

So what other journeys await us? More. Many more.

AMTRAK, THE ROAD BACK

*A*irports are terrible places, as far as I'm concerned. Granted, some are better than others, but any airport is basically over-crowded, too spread out, hard to park close to. The baggage seems to take forever to show up on the carousel, and people armed with back-packs and those folding little wheelie things are constantly bumping into everybody. There is little that could be called peaceful or even pleasant about today's airports. That's my principal reason for trying the trains.

For several years I have been enchanted with the train along the Hudson from Albany-Rensselaer to New York City. The seats are com-fortable. The passengers can walk around. The food is no worse than airlines', and you're not strapped in while you eat the stuff.

I decided to try a long trip on Amtrak. I boarded the train at bed-time one night in mid-December, bound for Colorado and Christmas. The porter was helpful with the luggage. A cunning little basket of wine and cheese awaited my arrival. The bed was comfortable even though this was an old Pullman car, the kind where the toilet disappears when the berth is lowered at bedtime.

Rhythm of the rails soothed my tired, fevered spirit and I wakened somewhere in Ohio for a pleasant breakfast and a relaxed view of the passing scene. By noon we were in Chicago with a four-hour layover. The accommodating redcap showed me where luggage was checked and promised to meet me in time to help me board the train to Colorado. I could have gone to the Art Institute, but I didn't realize I had that much time. The lounge for sleeper passengers was comfortable and quiet, anyway.

Out of Chicago my berth was in one of those glorious double-deckers—an economy berth with plenty of elbow room and a huge window. Dinner was a fine roast chicken. The conductor announced bingo games and movies in the lounge cars. Before breakfast, Reuben the porter brought juice, coffee, and the day's newspaper for my morning pleasure. We smiled and chatted. The whole trip was just fine. I was in La Junta, Colorado, at eight the next morning, being met by son Matthew. No crowds, no fuss, no waiting for luggage that won't show up.

The trip took thirty-six hours. I did some writing, some reading, and a lot of sleeping. The compartment was almost a decompression chamber, so I arrived ready for family and Christmas. The extra time was not wasted; it was my Christmas bonus to myself for the hard work I'd been doing, whatever that was.

Now I'm writing to my congressman to beg him to keep Amtrak on the rails. For women like us, the train is perfect for travel and would be a downright party for two or three traveling together.

*O*ne word about those travel companions, please: Choose carefully. I mean, carefully. Some of the nicest friendships I have known have failed to withstand the rigors of traveling together.

One reason is failure to spell out ground rules before leaving home, particularly about money. This might sound strange, but you'd be amazed at the way some of the "nicest" women we know can spoil a vacation by disagreeing about money.

Some people prefer less-expensive restaurants and Plain Jane hotels. Others consider the hotel and the food to be the major object of travel and want only the finest. Work that out before you even agree to go along, no matter how many years you and your proposed companion have played bridge every Monday at one-thirty. She might be a real wildcat when it comes to splitting a dinner check. Beware.

How long can I be away? How far should I go? How can I be contacted in case of emergency? How many overdue bills will I be faced with if I stay away too long? These are important questions. Personally, I dislike being out of touch with my family for more than a week at a time, at least by phone, and I always seem to beat my postcards home no matter how long I stay.

But send some postcards to yourself to add to your scrapbook, dated and with your comments for yourself.

One more travel tip, ladies: I could not believe a woman writer who visited me after a conference in Saratoga Springs. She prides herself on being a liberated, independent, feminist, activist woman-of-the-world. She had no idea how to go home to Washington.

It is not always necessary to stick to a rigid schedule, but *never* leave home without a fixed picture of the logical way to return to your home. Having round-trip plans could be called the prime requisite of successful travel for the single woman.

And speaking of returning home, have you noticed how many friends ask, "How was your trip?" and never wait for an answer? Don't be surprised. It happens all the time.

One solution for that problem is a travel club—just a little one. I know of groups of women who gather for lunch once a month just to talk about trips. They exchange observations and travel tips, and sometimes plan jaunts together. This often gets some of the shy ones out of the house and away from *The Edge of Night* or *Days of Our Lives* for a while. If you don't have a travel club or know of one, suggest to your agent that a travel club for older women would be a great service from her agency. She might let you be the president, or offer you a job.

Some travel agents welcome part-time tour directors who can get along with a crowd and plan excursions. We all learned a lot about that being den mothers; now we can put the experience to our own use. The normal arrangement is to work outside the office on a commission basis. Promotion of tours is the responsibility of the tour person, not the agency. This can fill time and bring in a little money, as well as afford the opportunity to travel yourself. After the first year, outside salesmen for travel agencies are entitled to agents' rates for personal travel. That's the best part.

My first trip to China was an agents' familiarization trip with my boss, Judy Smith. Later that same year we went to Sweden and the Scandinavian Waterways. I have sailed with Royal Viking both ways, as an agent escorting a group of passengers and as a private passenger. Either way is fine with me. Rates at hotels and resorts are lower for agents. You might have gasped when I mentioned keeping two grandsons at the Waldorf Astoria. Agents' rates, ladies. You can do it, too.

This tour business might be frustrating in the beginning, but it can be rewarding. You'll find yourself providing opportunities for women who are fearful of venturing forth on their own. When it comes to getting on the road, being an employee of an agency is worth the trouble.

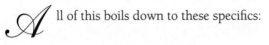 ll of this boils down to these specifics:

1. Don't carry anything. An eighty-eight-year-old woman who rides the buses regularly mails her clothes to the friend she's visiting. That's right—mails her clothes. Isn't that marvelous? She has no luggage to wrestle with or keep track of or wait for when it doesn't show up. Only a small purse goes with her. This is my best tip.

2. Plan carefully, but not too much. Just because you're going to Southern California, don't try to see all of your cousins, old neighbors, and childhood friends in four days while rushing through Sea World, Disneyland, and Universal Studios. Give yourself enough time (what's the hurry to get back to an empty house?) or concentrate on one or two purposes of the trip. Don't gather everyone you want to see into one big group. That spells disaster. Each wants to see you on your own.

3. Short excursions can get you in the mood for major-league travels. Most women fail to see the advantage of staying overnight on a jaunt to see a show or visit the museums in a near-by city. Take time. You have lots of that.

4. Learn to handle money like men do. This means, keep small bills and change in your pocket where it's easily available for taxis, tips, and such. On the street in New

York City in broad daylight I saw a kid grab the wallet from a young woman's handbag and race off through the crowd. That's when I started wearing only clothes with pockets while in transit. Besides, nothing makes a woman look older or more helpless than groping around in a nine-pound purse-satchel for a quarter.

5. Supply yourself with the right denominations of money. Stop showing up for lunch with nothing smaller than a twenty-dollar bill. We women tend to be content with the money that falls into our hands by chance—what the teller gives us when we cash the check or whatever comes in change at the sales counters. It's just as important to have small bills or coins as it is to carry your lipstick and pictures of the kids.

No matter how you do it, just get out there and *go!*
Have a good trip!

Support Groups

Join the Crowd!

I n the process of writing this book, I have used many words, some of them too many times. But not once have I used the word "happy."

Happy is not the point. Happy is the by-product of what we are discussing here. Quality of life is the business at hand. If yours brings happiness, that's fine.

Sam Levenson said, "God never promised Mamma happy," in his book, *In One Era and Out the Other*. I tend to agree. Happy comes from our own efforts.

Where do we look for improvement in the quality of our lives? First of all, within ourselves. We sit quietly with a pen and paper one day and make lists of "I can" and "I know" and "I have." Then we analyze the world in which we live. What are the other kids on the block who are your age doing these days? Where do they go? Does something in particular seem to work for the other older women in your church circle or in your line at the market? What's going on in town at your library or arts center? Or the YMCA?

e shy away from the term "support group" because that sounds like some outfit for sickies. Widows are not sick. We just need a sense of direction, a way to get rolling again in this new phase of our lives. Group counseling for grief therapy is readily available everywhere. Ask your doctor about that—or consult your daily newspaper. But for escaping from the humdrum ruts that seem to threaten us, help is accessible around every corner.

So far in the research for this book, and for the enhancement of my own life, I have sampled senior activities from lunch at SRDA in Pueblo, Colorado, to AARP in Hudson Falls, New York. In each instance, I was delighted to find men and women with vigor, enthusiasm, and a zest for living. In Hudson Falls there are four hundred members of AARP. Now, Hudson Falls is just as small a town as its name implies. But the *waiting list* for AARP is up to fifty. Meeting spaces can't hold the whole crowd. These people are busy planning trips to Nashville and other spots, contributing to community projects, and keeping up with legislation that affects oldsters.

At lunch in Pueblo, there was live music provided by a dandy ragtime piano and banjo. The food was fine, the crowd friendly and lively.

Don't be a snob about these places, ladies. Don't decide you're not old enough to need a new friend or two. Don't let the idea of being surrounded by our peer group once in a while shut you out of some good times.

I know many women who refuse to ask for a senior citizen's ticket at the movies or a senior discount, because of pride. That's foolish. Everyone is getting older. You're just ahead of the pack, right now. Nothing to hide about that. Let yourself take part in activities geared to our age at least once. Surprise yourself by finding kindred souls who are coping with the same mishmash facing you. Find out how others manage. That makes any group a support group.

The woman most adrift when she becomes a widow is the woman who is unprepared, even in her own head. She is probably the person who has said, "If I die"—generally the same type who has always been surprised by Christmas coming so soon. This lady is the weeper in the supermarket, convinced she is the only wife in the world whose husband was "taken from her." She's a special case, not to be dealt with here. We're talking about sensible people who have at least thought about facing the inevitable.

*B*ack to support groups:
Yours might be your bridge club if you work it right. That is, be open and honest about your feelings with close friends without monopolizing table conversation or haranguing the still-married players with your problems. My daughter plays bridge with seven women much older than she is. They keep track of each other. Understand each other. Now that it's more difficult for them to drive to take care of their own needs, the others are aware and helpful without trying to be nosy or dictatorial. But as chronic disease and really old age catches them, they need each other more.

Other "old crowds" are not as helpful, especially couples. One of the most miserable widows I have ever seen is a fifty-ish gal who expected to be included in everything the old gang did after she was alone. This sort of dependence is embarrassing for the old friends who are uncomfortable coping with an extra woman all the time. Five people in one car, for example.

Do not treat your old married friends as a support group. They'll try hard for a while, ladies, but many a long-lasting relationship has been wiped out by a third/fifth party always hanging around.

Farther afield are better support groups, even though we might not give them such a name. The local museum sponsors trips to bigger or other exhibitions. Most of the patrons are old ladies just like you. The library has programs of foreign films or readings by local poets and writers. Smart older women intent upon keeping their curiosities alive are to be found there. Your schools might need someone to help the children who cannot read. Other older people are doing that, too.

Best of all, your community college is a gathering-place for older people who recognize the advantages of learning more for their own satisfaction. State universities have programs *free* to senior citizens who want to audit courses. No need to study for a degree. You're learning to please yourself.

A while ago I saw my Spanish professor from Adirondack Community College and thanked him for such a good time in his class. I could not say even that in Spanish, of course, but he seemed gratified by my greeting anyway. Fellow students from that Spanish class have become fast friends. We do other things together now. The same holds true for classmates from anthropology and creative writing. We get together. Keep track of each other.

Travel, carefully chosen, can provide moral support. Institutions like the Smithsonian attract participants in their travel groups who are generally older, often women. This is learning, traveling, and making new friends all at once. Try signing on alone. You'll meet more people that way and the extra single charge is worth it. Two women side by side all the time on a cruise or other trips tend to be left to their own devices. On board ship or on buses you can strike up friendships with any number of women who are facing the same choices, the same headaches, the same opportunities you are. Some will become real friends. Others will be fine examples of what you don't want to be.

"Whoever thought we'd find ourselves back in the classroom—and loving every minute of it!"

That's the quote on the cover of the latest catalog from Elderhostel. In the Adirondacks I effected a turnaround in my own life by attending Adirondack Community College. Now I find out I can keep the process going in any state in the union or almost any country abroad. What I know about Elderhostel is worth sharing.

Elderhostel welcomes anyone sixty or older to attend one-week courses in colleges and other institutions of learning across the country. This has been going on for years. It's a big program. For ±$335 per week including room and board, you or I can study Greek Mythology at Mississippi State, Architecture of Cape Breton in Nova Scotia, the Pleasure of Poetry at the Potsdam campus of the State University of New York (SUNY), or American Indian Writers of the Southwest at the College of Santa Fe in New Mexico.

Languages, cooking, computers, archeology, religion, and crafts are included in the myriad of offerings for the same fee. And each fee entitles the student to three courses, not just one. Of course, dormitories are not like the Ritz, and cafeteria food is not like dining at the River Cafe, but the groups are like-minded people of our own age— which sounds like congeniality-plus to me.

Some oldsters I know attend regularly. Orel and Blossom Friedman even went to New Zealand with Elderhostel for three weeks and had a marvelous trip. One man in Glens Falls has taken about twenty sessions on various campuses and swears each was worthwhile. Friends who haven't done Elderhostel seem to have cousins or sisters who've "been there."

The best way to enjoy the freedom and independence of these older years is to keep our heads working, our imagination and curiosity alive. When we can start a new conversation with our grandchildren, when we have a different subject to bring up at the bridge table or out to lunch with the girls, when we understand more of the world around us—in other words, when our awareness is working—we are more interesting to our family and to ourselves. That is one of the keys to successful aging.

Sitting back and saying, "I don't want to know" or "I cannot remember any more, so I—" is writing our own sentence for really declining years.

This is my impression of Elderhostel after a week at the College of Santa Fe:

> "We're all in our places
> "With bright shining faces . . ."

There we were, all seated at our desks, coats piled on a chair in the back of the room, notebooks and ball-points at the ready. Back in the classroom. And the faces were bright and shining—all twenty-eight of us.

"Is this your first Elderhostel experience?" this tall, Ivy-League-looking man with a well-trimmed beard and a well-dressed wife said to me.

"Yes. I'm really looking forward to this week," I replied, thinking I should have worn a freshman beanie or some such identification.

"I've certainly heard a lot about Elderhostel. Have you been here before?"

"Not here," said the man. "But Barbara and I have attended other sessions in the Smoky Mountains, in Ireland, in Wales, on the East Coast. This must be about our seventh, I'd say."

"This is our fifteenth," the woman across the aisle chimed in. "Last one was to New Zealand. But we've been all over the United States. You should try the one on the Chesapeake Bay or Alaska."

"This is my first." This from a little lady on my left. "I was spending the holidays in Albuquerque with my son and his family and wanted to know more about this part of the country. I live at Leisure World in Silver Spring, Maryland, and it seemed silly to turn right around and go home after New Year's, but my children are busy, so I decided to try this."

Of course, I told her about my friends Grace and Ed at Leisure World, and we talked a little more about being the freshmen in the crowd. But we talked. That's the big thing. These folks are vigorous, eager, expansive, easy to meet, interesting people from all over the country. They came from Illinois, Florida, Connecticut, Ohio, Minnesota, and so on.

And they are retired. The men are retired military or professors or businessmen. Some of the wives have had careers of their own. Some travel all winter to various Elderhostels, others would be going straight home. Each one, without exception, had something valuable to add to any conversation. Each of these people was ready for the challenge and opportunity of a new course in a different college, with more to absorb about the area, the Indians, the Southwest culture.

Our class sessions were stimulating. I had a hard time keeping up with my note-taking because I wanted to record the remarks, questions, and comments of my classmates as much as the lecture. Elder-hostelers are good listeners, good learners, and a fine bunch for hanging around.

"Well, what happened at this college course of yours? Did you stay out too late and get locked out of the dorm? Did they have bed check every night at eleven? Was there a room inspection to be sure you hung up your pajamas? Did you eat macaroni and cheese for a week? Any Spam?"

Those are questions from the cynics of my world who cannot believe this enthusiasm for a return to campus life, even for a week or two. I'll admit we do get pretty set in our ways—spoiled, perhaps—by having our houses to ourselves at this stage of our lives. A dormitory is surely a change.

I've tried dormitory life in several settings, ranging from Skidmore to Oxford to the College of Santa Fe, in the past many years. Go for it. That's all I can say. College people and college programs are great for us oldsters. The cost is reasonable, the food acceptable, and the rewards are enormous.

At the College of Santa Fe there are Elderhostel groups in the dorm forty-eight weeks of the year. The college is geared for our set. "We appreciate these students," we were told. "You don't leave graffiti on the walls or play ear-splitting music 'til all hours of the night. You're more gentle with the Coke machines. You are responsive and eager in the classroom."

The young woman in charge of the program in Santa Fe is pleasant but not condescending. She answers questions, hands out maps and shopping advice, arranges a tour of the city, and suggests opportunities for observing "local color." But she did not herd us around like mindless inmates. We saw the Museum of International Folk Art in one big group, but we visited near-by pueblos and weavers in a caravan we organized on our own. Some of the class saw *The Taming of the Shrew* performed by the local repertory theater, with mixed reviews. Others of us watched Spanish gypsy dances and poetry in a wing of the Museum of Fine Art, which seems to be an ancient church. We all looked for Indians selling pottery and sampled New Mexican food on our own. In other words, these continuing-education planners leave time for enjoying surroundings as much as classroom experience.

"So what did you study, exactly?" Another common question.

Traditions in Conflict.
Mythology and Science Fiction.
Literature of the Southwest.

Those were the courses offered at the College of Santa Fe to the Elderhostel class of January 4–10, 1987. These are not the only courses ever offered there, but I felt lucky to have arrived for this curriculum. We had evening discussions of fiber arts, Indian traditions, and so forth, but in the classroom this was it.

The first course, taught by a Christian Brother, concerned the roots of the Western Tradition and made me realize how little I had retained from M&M History forty years ago. We thought through early exploration and settlement of the New World, the Industrial Revolution, and the rise of Marxism as well as various and sundry wars along the way, but the point of the course was the total effect of these events on our lives today. Somehow such considerations make a lot more sense now than in my freshman days at Colorado College. And the answers to "Where do we go from here?" are a lot tougher than before World War II.

We talked, listened, and learned, and some of the students argued with the professor, but not me. Brother Gregory teaches many Elderhostel classes and has his subject matter carefully organized for a five-day course. I wanted to hear what he had to teach us in his carefully prepared lectures too much to argue fine points about religion and all that.

What does Ulysses have to do with Buck Rogers or Darth Vader? That's what we discussed in our second course, Mythology and Science Fiction. Most of us admitted we care little for the science fiction popular today, but we didn't want to be old-fogy enough not to try to understand. Each civilization has similar myths of truth-seekers, floods, exile, and such, but it had never occurred to me that Isaac Asimov and Ray Bradbury were writing updated versions of the same tales. Now I want to read more science fiction. It really isn't as much trash as I had thought it was. Not all of it, anyway.

The third course introduced most of us to names like Scott Momaday, an American Indian writer who won the Pulitzer Prize and made "Native-American" writing respectable. This opened doors for many of my classmates about the beliefs, rituals, and customs of the Indians of the Southwest today.

Elderhostel is not the only organization offering continuing education for oldsters around the country. At Adirondack Community College, at Skidmore, at SUNY, all over the Northeast there are affordable college courses for any of us who want to be sure our heads work as long as the rest of our bodies. In the West it's the same. At Pueblo Community College, at the arts centers and the libraries, everywhere we turn, there's an opportunity to improve the quality of our lives by doing something different, learning something new. Let's try as many as possible.

Nobody can know too much or have too many friends. Maybe that's why Elderhostel had grown so rapidly from a single New England campus more than fifteen years ago to a world-wide network of colleges and other learning centers in all fifty states and most foreign countries. There are more old folks every day, getting older every day, and we need something to do—something to think about—besides Medicare and fretting about what our kids are doing on Sunday afternoons when we are at home alone.

We had graduation ceremonies on Friday night in Santa Fe. Nobody played a flute solo or offered words of advice to the departing scholars, but one of our new buddies conducted an excellent quiz contest, and the evening ended with a joke-swapping session appropriate for any dormitory crowd.

Next, I think I'll try SUNY/Potsdam for Spring Flora of the Adirondacks, and then maybe an English Country House.

And then . . .

And you can't find anything to do?

Come on now! This is a support group *par excellence!*

Now, About Writing . . .

"Starting to Write After Forty" is the title of the workshops I have conducted in the past ten years. I'm not much of an expert about writing, but I am fully qualified as far as the age requirement is concerned.

Constantly I hear from women who are fascinated by writing. They ask, "How can I get started?" "Who helped you?" "Should I have an agent?" "Where do you get your ideas?" and other such questions.

I have now considered these basics enough to distill the answers. Remember, these are only opinions based on my experience.

1. Talk to anyone you know who writes—for anything.
2. Check with your local librarian for information about writers' groups and workshops in your area.
3. Contact the community college or state university in your town—don't overlook private colleges, either—for writers' courses, particularly creative writing.
4. Write. Start a journal and add to it every day. This is

not a diary. The journal is what you think, how you feel about any subject in order to explore your own feelings and your own facility for putting yourself on paper.

5. Read magazines like *Writer's Digest* or *The Writer* for advice about markets and methods of reaching publishers. There are excellent workshops all over the country where recognized writers in their fields take time to share knowledge and teach skills to aspiring authors.

6. Try all kinds of writing. John Updike says one essential for creativity is discovering your own genre. Are you a poet? A novelist? A nonfiction columnist? An essayist? A writer of short stories? A research expert? You'll never be certain 'til you've given yourself a shot at each sort of self-expression.

7. Form a connection with some sort of a group of your choice. Since my own experience is my greatest resource for discussing this subject, and since I started writing absolutely on my own except for one faithful friend who filled in the blanks for me along the way, I can only tell you what works for me. The Santa Barbara Writers Conference was my first connection with other professionals in a group. This has proven to be such a useful week of education and inspiration that I have returned to Santa Barbara every June since 1978.

My other alliance with writers is different: The International Women's Writing Guild is open to all women connected to or by the written word. These are not necessarily published authors who attend the workshops. The newsletter reaches more than three thousand women across the country with news of local workshops, writing opportunities, and the work of individuals wanting to contact others interested in the same subjects. IWWG has an annual conference and retreat at Skidmore College in Saratoga Springs, New York, and can be contacted through Caller Box 810, Gracie Station, New York, NY 10028.

8. Learn all you can about small presses and smaller magazines. The market is there for magazine free-lancing. Thousands of magazines are published that you and I have never heard of. *Writer's Market* lists them according to topics of interest and fills in details about how to submit, what you might be paid, and all that. The market for nonfiction in periodicals is much larger than for fiction. Poetry is very hard to peddle, worse to make any money off of.

9. If you are really a neophyte writer, forget about finding an agent right away. Agenting is a complex, highly structured business. No agents take on magazine submissions as a general rule. The best way I can suggest is just keep going to workshops and conferences, to hone your writing skills and make connections. Then one day you will meet an agent interested in your work.

10. Finding a publisher is almost worse than establishing yourself with an agent, since the two are interdependent. Like that old song about love and marriage, you can't have one without the other.

No writer/columnist/housewife in Colorado can sit here and give you the exact formula for succeeding with a career or an avocation in writing. But I can tell you this: If you work hard enough and long enough, and are willing to accept some rejections along the way, you will find nothing in life more satisfying than seeing your own words in print, or being stopped in the supermarket or the lobby of the bank by someone who says, "I just want you to know I like what you write."

It's worth the trouble, believe me.

One fine example of that satisfaction of the printed word arrived in my mail this week. Talk about synchronicity. Nineteen oldsters who write in class together have compiled a book. I get to read some of it before the finished printing.

Judging from the mini-biographies with the text, these people write for the love of it, and for the love of life. Does any better reason occur to you?

In story-telling of the first order, these authors recount and re-live moments of their own past without drowning all of us in family sorrows or inside jokes. Betty Smith resurrects in any of us who ever had anything to do with wringing a chicken's neck (even spectators) the vision of some garish headless flapping creature. We nod and laugh about her story. Similarly, this same Betty Smith captures for/in her reader the reluctant anguish we experience in memorializing the Vietnam War.

Words carefully chosen, judiciously placed satisfy the reader as much as the writer. In these "senior adult" years we have the time to explore, the experience to commit to paper, and the wit to balance emotions necessary to make writing more than a pastime or an escape from boredom. We have the new-found (for most of us) ability to create from our own heads the sort of family recollections and biographical essays prized by our families and admired by our friends.

In your town senior adults write in community classes or work-shops because they want to. In Denver, this class gathers at Arapahoe Community College under the tutelage of Aleon DeVore. Their book, titled *Autumn Gold—with a Touch of Silver,* will be published by The Electrum Press in Littleton, Colorado, but I cannot say exactly when.

Why are older women fascinated by writing? I hear that question frequently. My answer: Until we reached this wondrous age, we had not enough time of our own to sit down in a quiet place, collect our thoughts, let our imagination and memory float free, and enjoy our own heads. Now we can do that, and we write.

A Newer View
of an Older You

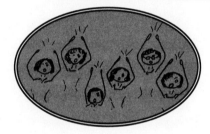

Twenty Per Cent Still to Go

"*A*ll the world's a stage, and you are not the first to play the part of Old Person. The audience has seen the play thousands of times and knows your lines better than you do. The role you are expected to play is not flattering. The Old Persons who have walked the boards before you have been crotchety, stingy, boastful, boring, demanding, and arrogant. They have complained of their illnesses and many other things. You may be surprised at how easy it is to play the part that way. The audience expects such a performance. . . ."

Wonderful paragraph, isn't it? That's from *Enjoy Old Age,* by Skinner and Vaughan, and it carries their book, or this one, in a nutshell.

Just who are you going to be for the last act, the last twenty per cent of your life? How much will the rest of your life characterize your feeling for life itself?

Albert Schweitzer often referred to a reverence for life. We need to pay attention there. Old people tend to give the impression they're just serving out their sentence, and you'd jolly-well better stay out of the way or wait on them hand and foot because they have put in so much time already.

When we were girls, we looked different, we dressed differently, we had aspirations and intentions almost unrecognizable these days. When we were girls the movies were censored, the music was hummable, the lyrics were memorable, the speed limit was sixty or seventy, Little Orphan Annie and Ovaltine Shake-Up Mugs were the biggest thing since sliced bread. We doted on *One Man's Family* and cried about Will Rogers and Wiley Post, or King Edward and Wally. We wanted to dance like Shirley Temple, sing like Judy Garland.

When we were teen-agers, we knew how many ration stamps were necessary for a bottle of catsup, if you could find any. We agonized over the newsreel pictures of the war in the Pacific or the Battle of the Bulge. We sang "Serenade in Blue" and "Deep Purple."

After the war, our skirt lengths went from the Dior New Look in the '50s to near-minis as we became new mothers, young matrons. We read Dr. Spock and endured Howdy Doody. Bantam League football and Junior League were the order of the day. As volunteers, we contributed to the world around us. Inside the family, we encouraged straight A's and the budding careers of our workaholic husbands.

Now here we are, you and I, ready to take on one more slice of life. But we are still girls. Deep inside us, warm and cherished, is the same person who has done the best she could through whatever came into her life. The face is changed. But the Girl is here—the Girl with the Grandmother Face, and the whole world is gonna be glad we're still around.